RELICS FROM THE CRUCIFIXION

J. CHARLES WALL

RELICS

FROM THE

CRUCIFIXION

Where They Went and
How They Got There

SOPHIA INSTITUTE PRESS
Manchester, New Hampshire

Sophia Institute Press
Box 5284, Manchester, NH 03108
1-800-888-9344

www.SophiaInstitute.com

Sophia Institute Press® is a registered trademark of Sophia Institute.

Library of Congress Cataloging-in-Publication Data

Names: Wall, J. Charles (James Charles)
Title: Relics from the Crucifixion : where they went and how they got there / J. Charles Wall.
Other titles: Relics of the Passion
Description: Manchester, New Hampshire : Sophia Institute Press, 2016. | Originally published under title: Relics of the Passion : London : Talbot, 1910. | Includes bibliographical references.
Identifiers: LCCN 2015039229 | ISBN 9781622823277 (pbk. : alk. paper)
Subjects: LCSH: Jesus Christ—Crucifixion. | Relics.
Classification: LCC BT465 .W35 2016 | DDC 232.96/6—dc23 LC record available at http://lccn.loc.gov/2015039229

CONTENTS

ILLUSTRATIONS

RELICS FROM THE CRUCIFIXION

The origin of the True Cross we cannot pretend to know, although it has frequently been accounted for in the romantic legends of all ages and Western nations during the Christian era. Its intermediate history, difficult to preserve through periods of semibarbarity, has been rendered still less trustworthy by the fabulous stories of itinerant pardoners of the Middle Ages,[1] who have done so much to confuse true relics with false that there are comparatively few that can be relied on. Except for a few fragments, the chief of these relics (the Cross) is lost, lost in the very efforts aimed at its preservation.

The wood of the Cross, however, forms such an integral part of the history of Christendom, and of those nations at one time adjoining her eastern limits, that the greatest skeptic cannot but acknowledge its influence. Whether it was the actual wood on which Christ died or a premeditated fraud of the emperor Constantine (c. 275-337) for political motives in no way alters the power it exercised.

---

[1]   In the Middle Ages, pardoners were preachers delegated to raise money for religious works by soliciting offerings and granting indulgences.

RELICS FROM THE CRUCIFIXION

The finding of the Cross immediately affected the Roman Empire, and a little later the whole of Europe, not only in religion and politics, but in literature and all branches of art. It has stirred men's minds as no other one thing has ever done, except the Divine Sacrifice. It created a fervor among Christians unknown and unequaled by any of the faiths of the world, not even excepting that of the Muslim. The Cross became the standard, not only of a creed, but of nations.

What if the whole story of the finding of the Cross was a fabrication?

This question is forced upon us when very many of our countrymen assert that such is the case. To determine this is no easy matter; much depends on the individual opinion of Constantine's character, his aims, and the state of the times.

Belief in the gods was fast decaying. Faith in them was almost dead, and, generally speaking, men possessed no religion. The Christians, although yet a very small minority, were growing in numbers and not to be ignored. They were a people knit together by a great invisible bond, whose courage had been proved in the arena, their loyalty on the battlefield and in the camp. Those who had shown a firmness exemplary even in the Roman army and whose honor had become proverbial, would naturally be appreciated by a wise general, even though members of a despised sect.

Constantine had doubtless learned from his mother, Helena (c. 246-c. 330), the high ideal of the Christian's life, even though he had not embraced the Faith. We know not how far St. Helena influenced him, but where there had once been persecution and oppression, under his rule there was free exercise of conscience. Although as yet he was not professedly a convert to Christianity, the faith of his mother had to a great extent worked into his soul, which, if not sufficiently grasped to control his passions, greatly guided his edicts.

Whether from political motives or not, we find the emperor recounts to Eusebius (c. 260-c. 340), bishop of Caesarea, a vision he professed to have had, in which the Cross was shown to be the symbol by which to conquer.

To conquer by the Cross! By the object of detestation to all Romans, concerning which Cicero says, "Let the very name of the cross be absent not only from the bodies of Roman citizens, but also from their thoughts, their eyes, their ears." By the instrument of punishment for slaves and felons, not only of the Romans, but also among Greeks, Carthaginians, Egyptians, Persians, and Assyrians. How utterly beyond the comprehension of the peoples of the empire, yet in the face of all this Constantine adopted that symbol as his standard!

The term *labarum* is usually applied to the new flag or standard of Constantine in contradistinction to its predecessors, but it would appear to have been no new name, for we read in Sozomen that Constantine commanded artists to *remodel* the standard called by the Romans *labarum*, to convert it into a representation of the Cross, and to adorn it with gold and precious stones. The labarum is thus described by Eusebius:

> Calling together the workers in gold and precious stones he [Constantine] sat in the midst of them, and described to them the figure of the sign he had seen, bidding them represent it in gold and precious stones. And this representation I myself have had an opportunity of seeing.
>
> Now it was made in the following manner. A long spear, overlaid with gold, formed the figure of the cross by means of a piece transversely laid over it. On the top

of the whole was fixed a crown, formed by the intertex-
ture of gold and precious stones; and on this, two letters
indicating the name of Christ, symbolized the Savior's
title by means of its first characters, the letter P being
intersected by X exactly in its center; and these letters
the emperor was in the habit of wearing on his helmet at
a later period. From the transverse piece which crossed
the spear was suspended a sort of streamer of purple cloth,
covered with a profusion of embroidery of most brilliant
precious stones; and which, being also richly interlaced
with gold, presented an indescribable degree of beauty to
the beholder. This banner was of a square form, and the
upright staff, the full extent of which was of great length,
bore a golden half-length portrait of the pious emperor
and his children on its upper part, beneath the trophy
of the cross, and immediately above the embroidered
banner."[2]

The Greek letters X (chi) and P (rho) form the monogram
of the name Χριστος, used in the earliest Christian symbolism
for Christ; and in the illustration of the labarum, on the reverse
of a coin of Constantine the Great, we see one of its first public
representations.

Thus, the Cross supplanted the eagle in the imperial standard;
otherwise it was the same as the old *vexilium* with the cloth fastened to the crossbar, although this also was embroidered with
Christian symbols.

[2] Eusebius, *The Life of the Blessed Emperor Constantine: From 306
to 337 A.D. : In Four Books*, The Greek Ecclesiastical Historians of the First Six Centuries of the Christian Era (London: S.
Bagster and Sons, 1845).

Fig. 1: Labarum on reverse of a coin of Constantine.

"By this sign, conquer!" In thus making the cross their stan-dard, Constantine enforced a reverence from the army toward the sacred sign. Tertullian tells us that "the camp religion of the Romans was all through a worship of standards," and in this way even unbelievers fought for and defended the Cross with their lives.

It was a bold stroke of the emperor, and it cannot have been but for divine guidance—perhaps communicated through a heavenly vision—that the Cross was thus raised from a symbol of ignominy to one for semi-adoration. How far this influenced the acceptance of Christianity will never be known, but surely there were many inquiring minds that would demand the reason for this exaltation of the Cross, and it may be surmised that it was frequently the initial step preceding the acceptance of the religion it represented.

The Cross did conquer.

Victory after victory was gained, until in 323 to 324 the Cross met the old eagle of Rome near Adrianople, where Constantine defeated Licenius, ultimately planting the Cross on the shores of the Bosporus.

With the Cross placed prominently before the world, at the head of the army, on the imperial diadem, and on the coins of the Byzantine Empire, combined with the freedom accorded to Christians for public worship, the Faith rapidly spread. The Romans and those nations conquered by her arms were now familiar with the sign of their redemption, and the people could fearlessly embrace the religion of the Nazarene. Then it would seem that Constantine determined to search for those relics, which might yet be spared, of the divine Founder of that Faith.

Now comes the act that the emperor is accused of playing solely for his own temporal ambition, at the expense of truth and honor. It is impossible definitely to accuse him of such contemptible behavior, although the lack of sufficient support in the evidence somewhat clouds his genuineness. If he could persuade the world that he had found the original Cross, it would at once consolidate the growing power of the Christians and raise their confidence in him to an enthusiastic height.

According to tradition, Constantine raised beacons at various points by which the result of the search could at once be transmitted to his capital. There the towers remain, with no history attaching to them, and of no account except to convey news from one part of the empire to another, a contrivance quite in harmony with the astuteness of a Roman conqueror. If, however, they were erected especially for news of the discovery of the Cross, as some native legends assert, these structures exhibit an unbounded confidence in the result of the explorations, which has strengthened the idea that the whole scheme of the discoveries was prearranged.

The silence of Eusebius is said to be fatal to the truth of the discovery; it certainly is inexplicable. He who wrote a detailed biography of the emperor and described the finding of the Holy Sepulcher would surely have recorded it had the instrument of our Savior's Passion been also found—an event of so great importance to the Christian world and which would redound to the honor of the sovereign. The story of the discovery of the Sepulcher went unchallenged by the learned of Jerusalem and by the numerous enemies of Christianity, whose knowledge of the locality would make them able and willing exposers of a Christian's fraud. Why, then, no record of the finding of the Cross?

That three crosses were brought to light cannot be doubted, and if they were not those of our Lord and the two thieves, the whole arrangement must have been preconceived by Constantine and his hirelings to impose on his aged mother, the Christians, and the empire.

The locality of the Sepulcher was well known to the Hebrews, whose attention to the burial places of their ancestors was proverbial. To think that the early converts would be an exception to this rule would be contrary to all reason, especially when it is remembered that the burial site was the human temple of their God, who had been laid there and who had risen from that tomb. The ruling power, hitherto antagonistic to their creed, had alone hindered a monumental mark. One other matter served to perpetuate the site, the very act intended to obliterate it: for that spot had been defiled by a temple dedicated to heathen deities, whose fame it was possibly supposed would eclipse any former association.

The absence of written records of the period between the Crucifixion and St. Helena's mission must not be taken as a proof that no record was made of the discovery; we know that vast numbers of works were written and that great libraries existed. We know as well of their irremediable destruction. Even had this not been the case, the oral traditions of the East were, and are, so generally accurate that they are oftentimes more reliable than many of the written works of the West. The earliest writing spared to us on this subject is from the pen of Cyril of Jerusalem (c. 313-386), about twenty years after St. Helena's discovery, since which time nearly all the extant works of the Fathers and of historians accept it as a historical fact.

The modern doubt as to the locality of Calvary, emanating, it would seem, from a desire to contradict former centuries of Christian tradition—even going so far as to discover an opposition tomb on another site—is discredited. The argument as to

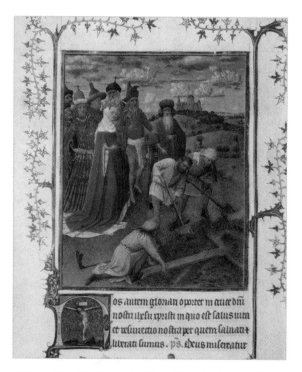

Fig. 2: The Finding of the True Cross by Jan van Eyck.

the true position rests on the direction of the *second* wall of Jerusalem. This, some people contend, included the accepted Calvary, whereas it was without the wall of the city. Recent research, however, upholds the site that has for ages been pressed by the knees of pilgrims who have gathered to pray by the Sepulcher of their Lord.

The arguments affecting the verity of the Holy Sepulcher also affect the Holy Cross.

While excavating for the Cross, the Sepulcher was first unearthed, and after further digging, the Holy Cross, the object of the expedition, with the crosses of the two thieves, were revealed to the gaze of the anxious explorers.

At one end of the Basilica of the Holy Sepulcher is a flight of steps leading down to the subterranean chapel of St. Helena, from which another flight descends yet deeper into the cavern, or chapel, of the Finding of the Cross.[3]

It was the custom of the Jews to burn the crosses used by the Romans for the execution of malefactors, but the haste observed on this occasion to get everything out of sight before the feast of the Passover readily accounts for these three crosses being thrown into the city ditch, or a hole, and buried from view, instead of the longer task of burning.

At the time of the discovery were also found Nails and the Spear.

---

[3] When this book was published in 1910, the feast celebrating the St. Helena's discovery of the Cross was still known as the feast of the Invention of the Cross. In the ensuing century, the meaning of the term *invention* shifted so much as to cause confusion in this context, so in this book we shall refer to that feast by a name less confusing: the feast of the Finding of the Cross or, sometimes, the feast of the Discovery of the Cross.

RELICS FROM THE CRUCIFIXION

The distribution of the relics said to have been found at once began. Constantine decorated his armor, his helmet, his sword, and his horse's bit with some of the Nails. Perhaps it would be more to the point to say that he armed himself against misfortune with these relics as amulets, or charms, for assuredly he looked upon them as such. St. John Chrysostom speaks of the practice of carrying small pieces of the Cross as amulets. The significance afterward applied to this decking with relics was but sentiment, a prototype of the symbolism so favored by Durandus and others in later times.

In the same spirit, the emperor placed a piece of the Cross in the equestrian statue that was used to represent him near the Golden Gate in Constantinople. To judge from the spirit of the times, echoed occasionally in the history of our own country, it was here enshrined so that the imperial figure should receive the outward appearance of that homage directly rendered to the holy wood, as well as to throw a protecting power over the city.

The wood of the Cross was at first divided, that it might honor by its presence Old Rome and New Rome (Constantinople) in addition to Jerusalem. It was afterward subdivided to such an extent that no Christian country lacked a fragment, not even the far-off Christians of St. Thomas in India. The wealthy bought it; the poor toiled to adore it; and the valiant fought for it. It was justly considered the most precious of princely gifts.

Charlemagne (c. 742-814) was offered rich presents as he passed through Constantinople, but his journey had been for the honor of Christ, and he refused gold and jewels but asked for relics of the Passion of our Lord and of His saints, and joyously received from the emperor one Nail, some Thorns, and a large piece of the Cross.

Relics from the Crucifixion

Hugh the Great (898-956), father of Hugh Capet, sent an embassy to King Athelstan (c. 894-939) of England, asking the hand of his youngest sister in marriage. Adulph of Flanders (d. 933), who was entrusted with this mission, brought innumerable presents of great value to give weight to his request. Among them were the spear of Charlemagne, reported to be that which pierced our Lord's side, and part of the Holy Cross enclosed in crystal, which was so clear that the color and size of the wood was discernible. A fragment from the Crown of Thorns also accompanied the gifts. Athelstan bestowed portions of the Cross and the Crown on his favored monastery of Malmesbury.

The same king also received the sword of Constantine the Great from the emperor Hugh the Great in the hilt of which was enclosed one of the Holy Nails.

The natural sequence of this prizing of sacred objects was that a monetary value was set upon them, until they were at last considered as valuable articles for barter. Baldwin II of Constantinople (1217-1273) raised money for his army by pawning relics in that city, while professional pardoners arose who gained a livelihood by trading with the same holy wares.

No doubt many spurious pieces of wood were sold as fragments of the True Cross through this lust of gain, encouraged by the eager demand for those things among the enthusiastic, and by the ease with which the credulous faithful could be overreached. Natural as it may be for people in all ages to strive after wealth, it must have been but a sorry Christian who would thus manufacture imitations of things so immediately associated with the death of our Lord and forge certificates of authenticity. Yet how can the present age say anything in condemnation of such practices, while Buddhas innumerable are turned out by machinery, in a Christian country, for the worship of devotees in the Far East?

It is this traffic that has in part shaken men's faith in relics of any description, and when it is found that the guarantees and seals of many are due to a cunning scheme of forgery, it gives free access to doubt.

Assertions are constantly made that there are enough relics of the Cross to build a ship, and again, that there is sufficient for the construction of a whole fleet. Perhaps the origin of such remarks may be found in the statement of Paulinus of Nola (c. 354-431), who said that however much might be cut away from our Lord's Cross, the bulk of the wood miraculously remained undiminished. The value, however, of all such sarcasms concerning the bulk of the wood is entirely lost when reference is made to M. de Fleury's careful investigation of all the attested fragments now existing, some of which are very minute.[4] He estimates that a cross, as used for execution, would contain about 6.29 cubic feet of wood, whereas the total of those pieces now extant amounts to only 0.14 cubic feet. How far would this go toward building one vessel, not to mention an entire navy!

The Church, of course, fulfilled her duty in appointing a day to commemorate such an event in the world's history as the Finding of the Holy Cross, as also year by year she observes the recovery (or exaltation) of the same wood that the Persians had seized. Yet this again is laid hold of by the doubter as an opportunity to inveigh against the verity of the relics.

The Cross thus found has been made the theme of epic poems. It has enriched the hymnology of the Church with some of her most precious compositions. It has been the cause of more bloodshed, in proportion to the population, than any other one

---

[4] Charles Rohault de Fleury, *Mémoire sur les instruments de la Passion De N.-S. J.-C* (Paris: L. Lesort, 1870).

thing in the history of nations. The contention for the Cross, even more than for the Holy Sepulcher, was the object of the earlier Crusades—those Crusades that drained Christendom of her blood while inspiring her sons with the highest motives. Expeditions worthily undertaken were to be, alas, the medium by which human passions, turned from their legitimate aims, were offered opportunities for the furtherance of personal animosity and selfish ambition.

Why should these pieces of wood so affect nations?

The Cross is more than the mere instrument of Christ's death. It is the figure and symbol of our Lord Himself. In the sight of the Christian, the Cross is most precious after the divine gift of Himself in the Sacrament of the Altar. How fully this was recognized in those crusading days is seen by its loss. Chosroes of Persia perceived this in the Christians' determined defense of it, and, when he seized that portion of the Cross kept at Jerusalem, he flattered himself that in it he possessed the Son of God, and he had it enthroned at his right hand.

The discovery of these relics led to inestimable results. It gave an impetus to all arts. The finest works since the classical period emanated from devotion to our Lord and were the result of a yearning to dedicate to Him all His gifts to us.

The need of cases in which to preserve these relics led to the making of shrines, in which precious metals, enamels, and gems were ungrudgingly used. An ivory tablet in the cathedral of Trier, of the sixth or seventh century, that probably formed one side of a reliquary, is supposed to represent the bringing of the relics of the Passion to Trier at the instance of St. Helena; they are enclosed in a casket held by two ecclesiastics.

Shrines containing such precious relics would, of course, be kept in churches and, in order that they should be worthy

Fig. 3: Ivory tablet depicting the bringing of relics of the Passion to Trier.

of the reception of them, gave birth to architectural concep-
tions unequaled in splendor by those lacking such treasures.
Rome's Church of the Santa Croce in Gerusalemme, built by
imperial edict, had even its foundations laid in earth brought
from Palestine. La Sainte Chapelle in Paris and St. Spinia
at Pisa are gems of art that chronicle self-sacrifice and love.
So it was with painting, needlework, and music, all of which
breathed a spirit of devotion sought for in vain in such works
of later centuries.

That piece of the Cross left in Jerusalem was captured by
the infidels and was fought for and regained by the Christians.
The setting up of the Kingdom of Jerusalem under the sway of
Godfrey de Bouillon (c. 1060-1100), Duke of Lorraine, its short
existence and final overthrow, is replete with interest. The al-
ternate loss and regaining of the precious relic until it ultimately
disappeared caused continuous strife and made that name by
which Jerusalem has been known — the City of Peace — appear
a paradox. A glance at the vicissitudes Jerusalem was subjected
to during the Christian era will enable us better to realize how,

by those vicissitudes, the lives of the Christians, drawn there by the power of the Cross, were governed for joy or grief.

In the time of our Lord, Jerusalem was in the hands of the Romans. For a short time the Jews regained it; but their own dissensions prepared the way for Titus (39-81) to bring it again beneath the Roman yoke in the year 70. For half a century Jerusalem may be said to have existed but in name, until the emperor Hadrian (76-138) built a new town on its site about the year 130. On the ground formerly occupied by the Temple was erected a temple to Jupiter, while a statue to one of their voluptuous deities, either Venus or Jupiter, was raised over the Holy Sepulcher.

With Constantine's recognition of Christianity, Jerusalem began a new chapter in its history. It was again raised to an episcopal see, at first suffragan to Caesarea, but afterward given its Patriarch by the Council of Chalcedon, in 451.

In 614 it was taken by the Persians, and the churches were destroyed.

In 628 Heraclius (c. 575-641), the Byzantine emperor, reconquered Syria, and the Holy Cross was exalted.

In 637 it was captured by the Arabians under Omar (577-644). The Christians were treated with leniency and allowed to remain by paying a poll tax. The Western Empire sent contributions for the support of pilgrims, and the caliph Harûn-er-Rashîd (763-809) is said to have sent the keys of the Church of the Holy Sepulchre to Charlemagne.

In 969 it fell into the hands of the Egyptian Fatimites.

During the latter part of the eleventh century it was harried by the Turkomans; and the Christians, both residents and pilgrims, were fearfully maltreated. Among them was Peter of Amiens (1050-1115), known as Peter the Hermit, who was instrumental in bringing about the Crusades.

The city was in the hands of Iftikhar ed-Dauleh, a dependent of Egypt, when it was invested by the Western armies. On the fifteenth of July 1099, the Franks entered Jerusalem and wrought ample vengeance on its defenders. It was then formed into a kingdom with Godfrey as king.

In 1187 Yusef Salah ed-Din (c. 1137-1193), known commonly as Saladin, captured the city, but treated the Christians with great leniency. In 1229 it was surrendered to Emperor Frederick II (1194-1250). In 1239 it was taken by the emir David of Kerak, but four years later it was given up to the Christians by treaty.

In 1244 the Kharismians took the city by storm. Since that time it has remained in the hands of Muslims, although not to rest from those changes that had so torn her for centuries. In 1517, 1831, and 1840, it successively passed to Turks, Egyptians, and Turks, and, as of this writing in 1910, Muslims yet hold and reign over that which should be the center of Christianity.

That fated city! When its inhabitants clamored for the fearful curse — "His blood be on us and on our children" (Matt. 27:25) — they knew not what they did.

And the fate of that portion of the Cross kept at Jerusalem is shrouded in oblivion. Whether or not the novelist Martin Tupper (1810-1889) had authority for his theory he tells us not. Perhaps it was but to help clothe the plot of his novel that he made the crusader Hugh Langton (c. 1150-1209), father of the Archbishop of Canterbury, tear a fragment from the wood of the Cross with his teeth, as it was taken from the custody of the Christians at the battle of Tiberias. He says that the whole of it was burned save the mouthful that was afterward divided into seven pieces, the only remaining fragments of our Savior's Cross. True or not, it must be borne in mind that his theory affects only that beam which was kept at Jerusalem and leaves untouched those pieces distributed over Christendom.

Many have been the conjectures as to the sort of wood used for the Cross. Numerous are the legends connected with its origin; and the simple piety of some of the English peasantry, even to the present day, hinders their thoughtless use of the wood of certain trees to which these traditions are attached. What superstition! Yet how it rebukes those who are so enlightened as to speak familiarly of holy things until all reverence of any description is expelled from such natures.

There is but little doubt that the form of our Lord's Cross was not such as is understood by the *Latin cross*, but of the form of the Greek Tau, that is, like a simple block-letter *T*. We have the authority of St. Jerome (c. 347-420) and Origen (c. 184-254), Lucian (c. 125-180), and Tertullian (c. 155-c. 240), and the present shape appears to have been assumed only as late as the fourth century. The presumption that the Tau was then the customary form of the Cross is strengthened by the representations seen on amulets, reliquaries, and tombs of the third century.

The miraculous powers attributed to the Holy Cross are endless. After St. Helena's discovery, the first miracle was the healing of a sick woman, thus asserting it to be the True Cross as distinguished from the other two, and the records of the exhibition of such virtues is continuous for centuries.

Tradition says, that when Chosroes (c. 570-628), king of Persia, pillaged Jerusalem, God, by His omnipotence, transported a chest of incorruptible wood—made by the immediate followers of the Apostles and filled with relics from Jerusalem—by way of Africa to Cartagena, Seville, and Toledo, and from thence with the Infant Don Pelayo (d. 1153), to the sacred mountain near Oviedo, and finally to the Cathedral of San Salvador. By the command of the sovereign Alonzo the Great, it was opened in the presence of a number of prelates, who found that it contained portions of the following relics: the rod of Moses, the manna that fell from heaven, the mantle of Elijah, bones of the Holy Innocents, the branch of olive that Christ carried at His entry into Jerusalem, a great part of the True Cross, eight thorns from the Crown, the *Sanctissime Sudario* (or napkin stained with Christ's blood), the reed that He bore by way of a scepter, His garment; a relic of the Blessed Virgin, and one of the three crucifixes said to have been carved by Nicodemus.

In the Church of St. Saturnin at Toulouse is an enameled *châsse* (or reliquary box) of the twelfth century, on which is depicted the wonderful translation of a piece of the Cross from the Abbey of Josaphat, in Palestine, to Toulouse.

A mass of legendary lore has grown around these sacred relics. The following, given in the words of Roger of Wendover (d. 1236), will be an example of those legends composed and credited in the Middle Ages. It was in 1217, when the army of Louis IX of France went to the relief of the Castle of Montsorel:

> At the town of Redbourn in Hertfordshire the French soldiers pillaged the Church of St. Amphibalus, and stripped the monks, even to their inner clothing; they also took the relics of the saints from above the great altar and polluted them with their impious hands. One among them seized on a silver and gold ornamented cross, in which was contained a piece of our Lord's Cross, and hid it in his wicked bosom unknown to his companions; but before he had left the oratory he was possessed by a devil, and fell down grinding his teeth and foaming at the mouth. Then quickly rising, at the instigation of the devil,

he endeavored to strike at those around with his sword; they, however, pitying his agony and not knowing the cause of it, tied his hands and took him to the Church of Flamstead in a state of the wildest frenzy. As these robbers were entering that church for the purpose of pillage, they were met by the priest, clad in white vestments, who came forward to check the evil disposition of those impious men; but they, being alarmed about their mad companion whom they had brought with them, refrained from plunder, and there, in presence of their leader and many others, the aforesaid Cross leapt forth from the madman's bosom and fell to the ground.

The story goes on to say that they confessed how the Cross had been obtained, and for fear of the evil spirit possessing others, they restored it to its former sanctuary.

In addition to the Cross, there are other relics of the Passion—the Nails, the Crown of Thorns, the Spear, and some of the Sacred Blood—preserved to the present time.

How these precious relics passed from the custody of one to another, and how widely they were distributed, may partially be gathered from medieval wills, which frequently contain such bequests as below.

> ► *In the Will of Elizabeth*, Countess of Northampton, dated 1356: "I do will to the church of Friar Preachers, London, the cross made of the very Cross of our Savior's Cross, wherein is contained one of the thorns of His crown."

> ► *The Will of Thomas*, Earl of Warwick, dated 1369: "To the Bishop of Lichfield a cross of golde, wherein

part of the very Cross of Christe's Cross is contained, enameled with the arms of England."

- *The Will of Thomas*, Earl of Oxford, 1371: "To Maud, my wife, all my reliques now in my own keeping, and a cross made of the very Cross of Christ's cross."

- *The Will of Phillippa*, Countess of March, 1378: "To Edmund, my son, a gold ring with a piece of the true cross, with this writing, '*In nomine Patris et Filii et Spiritus Sancti. Amen.*'"

- *The Will of William of Wykeham*, Bishop of Winchester, 1403: "I bequeath to my church at Winchester, one cross of gold with relics of the Cross of our Lord."

THE ORIGIN OF THE WOOD OF THE CROSS

When the world rang with the news that the Holy Cross had been discovered, and everyone was asking for details, according to the working of each individual mind, there arose these questions among others:

Of what wood was it made?

Where did it grow?

In which locality budded forth that plant that, when matured, was to become the instrument of torture and the crude deathbed of the Son of God, the Son of Man, and the means of the world's salvation?

The cursed tree!

The blessed tree!

Not only were these questions asked, but every one was answered! Many were the traditions that sprang up for that purpose, never thought of before the great discovery of St. Helena.

The widespread legend of the origin of the wood that is found partly related in the apocryphal *Gospel of Nicodemus* (not later than the third century) and in the *Golden Legend* is to this effect: when Adam fell sick, he sent his son Seth to the gates of the

Garden of Eden to entreat God for some drops of the oil of mercy distilled from the Tree of Life with which to anoint his head. Seth easily found his way to the goal, as no grass had grown over the footprints of Adam and Eve since their expulsion. While Seth prayed at the gate, St. Michael appeared to him, saying, "I am sent unto thee from the Lord; I am appointed to preside over human bodies. I tell thee, Seth, do not pray to God in tears and entreat Him for the oil of mercy wherewith to anoint thy father Adam for the headache; because thou canst not by any means obtain it until the last day and times, namely, till five thousand and five hundred years be past."

Michael gave him, however, a branch of this tree, which, on the death of Adam, Seth planted on his grave. In after years, the tree flourished and attained a great age. When Balkis, the queen of Abyssinia, came to Solomon, she worshipped this tree, "for," said she, "thereon should the Savior of the world be hanged, and that from that time the Kingdom of the Jews should cease." On hearing this, Solomon commanded that the tree should be cut down and buried in a certain place in Jerusalem, where the pool of Bethzatha was dug, and the guardian angel of the mysterious tree troubled the waters of the pool at certain seasons, and those who first dipped into it were cured of their ailments (see John 5:1-9).

As the time of the Passion of the Savior approached, the wood floated to the surface of the pool, and of that timber was made the upright part of the Cross. The crossbar was made of cypress, the piece to rest the feet upon was of palm, and the inscription was written on a piece of olive.

Another common form of the same legend makes the archangel Michael, who refused Seth the oil of mercy, give Seth three seeds from the Tree of Knowledge to be placed beneath the tongue of Adam when he was buried, promising him that from those seeds should grow a tree that would bear fruit whereby Adam should be saved and live again. From the three seeds sprang a trinity of trees of three separate woods, cedar, cypress, and pine, although united in one trunk. From this tree Moses cut his rod. It was transplanted by David to the borders of a pool near Jerusalem, and beneath its branches he composed his psalms.

Solomon had it cut down to form a column in his Temple, but being too short, it was rejected and cast over a stream to serve as a bridge. The queen of Sheba, when visiting Solomon, refused to pass over on that tree, declaring that it would one day occasion the destruction of the Hebrews. The king ordered that it should be removed and buried. This was done near the pool of Bethesda, at which time the virtues of the wood were immediately communicated to the waters. After the condemnation of Christ, it was found floating on the surface of the pool and the Jews took it for the main beam of the Cross.

The prevailing idea was that the Cross was formed of three or more woods; either that the various parts were made, each from one of the three in that trinity springing from one root or, an idea not consistently followed, that the three woods were amalgamated, forming one trunk, out of which the upright beam was fashioned, thus containing in one beam the qualities of the three plants. And again, this peculiar growth was produced from three seeds containing three properties, although the fruit of one and the same tree.

It is curious to see how the same traditions will last through ages, taken from or added to, until in the last edition the earliest form is unrecognizable. Even Mandeville (fourteenth century) must have had very simple faith in the tradition—by his time much confused — to speak in his travels of a tree that was then lying as a bridge over the Kedron "of which the Cross was made."

The Venerable Bede (c. 673-735) and John Cantacuzenus (c. 1292-1383) both record the idea that the Cross was composed of four kinds of wood: cypress, cedar, pine, and box.

Innocent says the upright was of one wood, the transverse beam of another, the title of a third, and that the feet were supported on a projecting step made of a fourth wood.

In England a notion existed that the wood was mistletoe, then a tree, but that ever since the Crucifixion it has been but a parasite.

The aspen leaf was said to tremble because the Cross was of that wood.

In some parts of England the elder tree is supposed to have been the wood of the Cross, and to the present day some reverend peasants carefully look through their faggots before burning them for fear there should be any of this wood among them.

Another common idea is that the main beam of the Cross was of cedar, the transverse of cypress, the inscription was carved on a piece of olive, and the footrest was of palm.

Some people who meditate on the fabulous combine the woods of the fir pine and box in the Holy Cross. An old legend makes out that the Cross was made of "Palm of Victory," "Cedar of Incorruption," and "Olive for Royal and Priestly Unction." And in a Latin verse we are told:

> The foot of the Cross is Cedar,
> The Palm holds back the hands,
> Th' tall Cypress holds the body,
> The Olive in joy is inscribed.

Lipsius (d. 1606), the most learned writer on the subject, thinks that the Cross was probably of oak, a wood abounding in Palestine, easily procured and strong. The relics he had seen he thought to be of that wood.

It is pronounced to have been of oak by A. F. Angelo Rocca Camerte in his book *De Particula ex Pretioso et Vivivico Ligno Sacratissimae Crucis* (Rome, 1609), in which he gives an account of a fragment in the Apostolic Treasury. This is supposed to be the same fragment for which Pope Leo the Great (c. 400-461) thanks Juvenal (d. 458), bishop of Jerusalem, in one of his letters, circa 450.

Curzon says that all the very ancient relics of the Cross that he had seen were of the same wood, which had a peculiar, half-petrified appearance. In his possession were two relics, said to be of the True Cross, the older enclosed in a shrine of the late thirteenth century; the other, in a modern setting, was of a different wood.

So much for the divided opinions concerning the wood of the Holy Cross, which after all, with the multiplicity of conjectures, leaves the question unsolved. The folklore of Europe teems with them; certain veins of legends are found to run through countries where the same traditions predominate.

The fragments this writer has seen are of a rich burnt-umber color; the grain, a little lighter, stands somewhat in relief from the decaying fiber around, but the substance of them is too far perished to decide on the kind of wood they originally were.

Where did the wood of the Cross grow? King David is said to have transplanted it from Lebanon to a spot near Jerusalem. "To the west of Jerusalem is a fair church where the tree of the Cross grew," says Sir John Mandeville around 1360.

Relics from the Crucifixion

Henry Maundrell (1665-1701), in his description of a Greek convent that he visited about half an hour's distance from Jerusalem, says: "That which most deserves to be noted in the convent is the reason of its name and foundation. It is because there is the earth that nourished the root, that bore the tree, that yielded the timber, that made the Cross. Under the high altar you are shown a hole in the ground where the stump of the tree stood."

A mile or two west of Jerusalem, in a valley among the hills, is the Greek monastery of the Holy Cross, which is the convent referred to by these two travelers. The foundation dates from a period not long subsequent to the discovery by St. Helena. The buildings now standing are of a great age.

3

THE FINDING OF THE CROSS

The fourth century was a brilliant time in the annals of the Church. It was an age of great saints and Fathers; councils were held and heresies condemned. In this century Constantine saw that world-renowned vision, as we are told by Eusebius, which, as we have seen, so greatly influenced the pagan world.

In the year 326, St. Helena made her pilgrimage to the Holy Land, being over eighty years of age. Whether sent by her son for the furtherance of a scheme, or for the genuine wish to preserve holy places, or whether it originated in her own desire when plunged in grief for the tragic death of her beloved grandson Crispus (d. 326), we can never know. Whatever the origin of the journey, which must have been a wearisome undertaking for one of her age, especially with the mode of travel then in vogue, no one has yet dared to doubt the sincerity and devotion of the empress-mother, whom tradition fondly makes a native of Britain. The work she had undertaken required no mean energy; the accumulation of two centuries covered the traditional site of the Holy Sepulcher. In A.D. 136, the emperor Hadrian, in his efforts to banish Christianity and to remove all landmarks that would recall that religion to the minds of his people, buried Calvary with earth and erected on the eminence a temple to Venus.

The earliest account we have of the exploration on this spot is by Eusebius, who, however, mentions nothing about finding the Cross, nor is it quite certain whether it is the Cross or the Sepulcher that is alluded to in the letter of Constantine to Macarius (d. c. 330), bishop of Jerusalem:

> *Victor Constantine Maximus Augustus, to Macarius of Jerusalem*: Such is the grace of our Savior that no supply of words seem to be adequate to the expression of its present manifestation. For that the monument of His most Holy Passion, long since hidden under the earth, should have lain concealed for a period of so many years, till, through the destruction of the common enemy of all, it should shine forth to His own servants after their having regained their freedom, exceeds all admiration.... It is now my chief care that we should adorn with magnificent structures that hallowed spot which by God's appointment I have disencumbered of a most disgusting appendage of an idol, as of some grievous burden; which was consecrated indeed from the beginning in the purpose of God, but has been more manifestly sanctified since He has brought to light the evidence of the Savior's Passion.[5]

---

[5] Socrates, *The Ecclesiastical History of Socrates, Comprising a History of the Church, in Seven Books: From the Accession of Constantine, A.D. 305, to the 38th Year of Theodosius II, Including a Period of 140 Years*, translated from the Greek with some account of the author and notes selected from Valesius (London: G. Bell, 1879), 36-37.

The Finding of the Cross

It is probable that the mention in this letter of the "finding the monument of His most Holy Passion" alludes to the finding of the Cross and not of the Sepulcher; if this is so, it is the first mention extant of the discovery of the instrument of our Redemption. But in the *Itinerarium Burdegalense*, a record of a journey to Jerusalem in 333, seven years after the alleged discovery, no reference is made to the finding of the Cross; which great fact would surely be known to one who writes of the church built over the place of Resurrection. The silence of those contemporaries who had every opportunity to spread abroad and exult in so important an event throws some doubt on the tradition.

The first definite mention of the finding of the Cross is in the *Catecheses* of Cyril of Jerusalem, published more than twenty years after Helena's pilgrimage. Cyril, at the time of the alleged discovery, was a boy living in Jerusalem and would most probably have known at the time if the precious wood had then been found. When writing, he mentions it as an acknowledged fact and relates how fragments cut from the Cross were then spread over the whole world. He also refers to the finding in a letter to Constantine's son Constantius.

From the beginning of the fifth century until the Post-Reformation period, the truth of the finding of the Cross is undisputed.

We have seen how St. Helena, at a venerable age, made a toilsome journey to Jerusalem; she was empowered by the emperor to act according to her own discretion, and we know how she had the cooperation of the bishop of Jerusalem, Macarius. It is related by St. Gregory of Tours (573-595) that with the aid of a Jewish man named Judas, afterward baptized with the name Quiriacus, the site of Calvary was made known to St. Helena.

The resident Christians had told Helena that as the Crucifixion occurred on the eve of the Sabbath, the crosses and all traces of the execution had been hurriedly removed; that the crosses had been thrown into a pit that was under the ledge of rock, the place of Crucifixion, and, being unclean things and not to be touched, they had been covered over, where they would probably still be found. It is supposed that the Hebrews' custom was to burn the crosses on which malefactors under the Romans had suffered, and there was no reason—humanly speaking—why an exception should made in this instance except on account of the press of time.

The superimposed earth was removed, the Holy Sepulcher was discovered, and with further search the three crosses were found lying nearby; and close to them was found the tablet on which was written the inscription that Pilate had commanded to be fixed above the head of Christ.

In her perplexity over which of the three crosses had been the altar of the Divine Sacrifice, St. Helena consulted Macarius, who caused them to be successively placed against a Christian lady of noble family then lying at the point of death in Jerusalem. The two crosses first applied were of no avail, but at the touch of the third, the sick woman was immediately healed. Sozoman (c. 400-c. 450) tells us that, to confirm this miracle, a dead man was instantly restored to life by the touch of the Cross. On the other hand, Sts. Chrysostom (c. 349-407) and Ambrose (c. 340-397) say that the tablet with the inscription was yet fixed to the Holy Cross, which would allow of no doubt as to that on which our Lord suffered.

However this may have been, we can imagine how the news flew with fiery tongue from Jerusalem to Constantinople. From the tower of David on Mount Zion in Jerusalem the beacon signal was flashed to Ramah, to the hill of Omri, the heights of Lebanon, Berytus, Tripoli, and Antioch; across the gulf to

The Finding of the Cross

Tarsus, Mount Taurus, Laodicea, Sardis, and Pactolus. Along the islands of the Aegean Sea to the hills of Lesbos, Mount Ida, and Olympus, which declared to the inhabitants of Imperial Constantinople that the Cross was found. Before the news could be fully realized in Jerusalem, it was known in Constantinople! That primitive telegraph enabled the rejoicings of Christians in those far-apart cities to be celebrated at one and the same time. *Te Deum laudamus* (God, we praise You) simultaneously arose in the churches in view of the blazing path, and how many a *Dimittis* would also be murmured.

Some of those crumbling towers still stand on the mounts and headlands, and although no written record of their use has been left, the native tradition is that they were built by order of Constantine as signal towers to convey the news of the discovery from Jerusalem to Byzantium.

The greater part of the Cross — the upright beam — was encased in silver and entrusted to Macarius and his successors to be kept in the church that St. Helena built over the place of Crucifixion, which was dedicated in the year 335. Part of the Cross, with the Nails found at the same time, were sent to Constantine.

> *Our Lord then sent an angel wise*
> *and bade her divide it in four parts:*
> *the one should in the Temple bide;*
> *to Rome men should the other send;*
> *to Alexandria to bear the third;*
> *the fourth in her company home*
> *to Constantine with her to wend.*
> *And all this did, that lady's hand.*
>
> *In four pieces they it smote*
> *of the which God did know.*

RELICS FROM THE CRUCIFIXION

They did right with two as God meant:
to Rome and Alexandria them sent.
The third they left in that city,
as in a place of authority.
The fourth led they with Helen
unto her son King Constantine.
To meet her rode many barons
with great and fair procession
within the kirk of Saint Sophie.[6]

So important an event as the finding of the Cross, an event that thrilled through the veins of Christendom and made each individual Christian rejoice, demanded a day for its special commemoration: a day on which all the faithful should concentrate their thoughts and thanksgivings for that which was consummated on that wood; a day that throughout all ages should live after the greater part of the sacred tree was lost. September 14, the day on which it is supposed the Cross was found, was appointed for its annual observance.

For three hundred years, the main beam of the Cross was in the custody of the bishops of Jerusalem and was annually exposed on Easter Sunday to the pilgrims who thronged the Holy City.

At various times during this period, people of wealth were permitted to purchase small fragments, which were carried to Europe and placed in monasteries and churches, where they were received with unbounded joy and reverence. Gregory the Great (c. 540-604) sent a piece, enclosed in a reliquary cross, to Recaredo (c. 559-601), the first Christian king of Spain, circa

---

[6] *How the Holy Cross was found by St. Helen*, Fairfax MS. 14, Bod. Lib.

586; which is one of the most authentic records of the early distribution of the relics.

In 614 Chosroes II, king of Persia, descended upon Syria. Jerusalem was taken, ninety thousand Christians were put to the sword, and the Church of the Holy Sepulchre was destroyed by fire. Many prisoners were led into captivity, among them the Patriarch Zacharias. After some years of uninterrupted success the Persian monarch retired beyond the Euphrates, bearing with him the True Cross, naturally considered a great trophy even by a pagan army, seeing how the Christians valued it and how it had inspired their warriors to fight for it. Chosroes had a throne made for the sacred wood, which he placed at the right-hand side of his own, for in its possession he flattered himself that he held in bondage the Son of God.

The Cross had been valiantly defended, but the fierce on-slaught of those countless hordes of fanatics was irresistible, and, as the last defender, a Greek, fell, the Cross was seized by the infidels. That Greek, legend says, was a giant, who appeared among the garrison of Jerusalem, unknown to anyone. In the weakest point in their ranks, in the thickest of the fight, was seen the unknown. He had fought steadfastly all the day, and with his own arm he had slain a hundred of the rabble foe. Wherever he appeared the enemy fell like grain before the sickle. Retreating slowly, he had at last stationed himself at the door of the Chapel of the Cross; within the chapel the priests were bowed in prayer, and here for a long time his single arm kept back a host of the enemy. Driven at length within the walls, he stood erect at the foot of the Cross, now visible to the eyes of the foe, and when the praying priests had been hewn to the ground he stood alone to fight for the wood of Christ's suffering. The infidels shrank aghast from the eyes that flashed through his helmet; they were as the eyes of an avenging angel. Lifting between his clasped hands the cross hilt of his sword, he offered a prayer to Him for whom he fought, and Christ sent down His angels to be with him in the conflict. In vain the enemy pressed upon him; one sweep of his sword and the altar was ready for other victims. The night closed in, and none could approach the Cross, for the stout warrior, with God's help, yet guarded it; and when the gloom was too thick for foe to distinguish foe, they left him there, alone, triumphant, to the company of God and His angels. In the morning he was gone, and on the floor of the chapel they counted of those slain by his hand twelve of their chiefs and forty-four of the stoutest soldiers of the guard of Chosroes. Men might well say it was St. Michael the Archangel himself.

One of the most complete pictorial descriptions of the finding of the Cross is within our own land. On a sculptured cross, now fixed against the chancel wall of St. Helen's Church, Kelloe, Durham, is represented the finding of the Cross.

Fig. 4: Kelloe Cross depicting the finding of the True Cross.

The Finding of the Cross

It is a broad shallow Norman cross of stone, six feet four inches high, the shaft being shouldered beneath the cross-head, which was connected by a circle. Across the transverse arms of the cross is the legend *In hoc vinces* (In this sign).

The neck of the shaft contains an angel appearing to St. Helena in a dream, revealing the spot of the hidden treasure. In the central compartment beneath are two coroneted figures: one is Constantine holding a cross, and the other is St. Helena grasping a reliquary or casket. These are placed beneath an ornate floriated arch.

At the base is the Holy Cross. St. Helena with a drawn sword (emblematic of the force of the regal authority) gives Judas an alternative: reveal the spot or die. At the other side is Judas in a turban with a spade. At their feet lie two corpses, and another figure, restored to life by the miraculous touch, disengages herself from the grave clothes to adore the symbol of Life.

4

THE RECOVERY OF THE CROSS

The emperor Heraclius at last declared war against Persia in 622. After three successful expeditions, the tide was turned and Chosroes was defeated in 627. He was ultimately deposed and put to death by his son Siroes (590-628) in the following year.

Siroes succeeded to the throne for the short reign of one year, during which time a peace was concluded. One of the conditions insisted upon by the Christians was the restoration of the Cross. This was conceded, and when Heraclius returned to Constantinople, the triumph of his entry was concentrated in the Cross, which was borne by four elephants before his chariot.

In the following spring, the emperor made a pilgrimage to the Holy Sepulcher for the purpose of restoring the Cross to its former sanctuary. The patriarch had recognized his own seals unbroken on the case, or shrine, enveloping the relic, by which he knew it had not been tampered with during its exile among pagans. It was said that Sira, the queen of Chosroes, who countenanced Christianity, had been the means of safeguarding it from profanation.

As the emperor approached Jerusalem with his precious charge, he recalled the humility of Him on whose shoulders it had been laid, and with all lowliness he divested himself of his imperial vestures. With uncovered head, bare feet, and clad only in a peasant's cloak, he carried the wood on his own shoulders back to Calvary. In some of the martyrologies, it is said that the emperor was miraculously restrained by an invisible power from proceeding with the Cross until he had discarded all attributes of royalty.

The day of the restoration of the Cross to Jerusalem was the feast of the Exaltation, September 14, 629.

There was peace in Jerusalem for but eight years. The Arabian power had rapidly grown, and once again the city fell before the overwhelming invasion of Omar in the year 637. With a magnanimity wholly unexpected from the Muslims, a special edict permitted the Cross to remain in the possession of the Christians in Jerusalem, whose presence was tolerated on payment of a poll tax. Throughout the year, and more especially on the great festivals, pilgrims still thronged the approaches to the city, and, although their worship had to be carried on with less ostentation, they were allowed to conduct their services within the walls of the churches; but outdoor processions were forbidden, bells were not to be rung, only tolled, and clergy and laity were not permitted to wear crosses publicly.

The fratricidal quarrelings of the Muslims proved of assistance to the Christians, seeing that the Muslims' own disputes occupied their minds too fully to allow interference with another religion. The constant wars of Harûn-er-Rashîd and his house with the emperors of Constantinople were also a means of benefit to the Christians of the Holy Land, as their conquerors, dreading lest the Eastern armies should call the Westerns to their aid, showered upon them every possible mark of favor. In 969 the Egyptian Fatimites again made the state of the Christians so unbearable that in the following year, John I of Constantinople (c. 925-976) attempted to free Palestine from Muslim power. All was favorably progressing until the leader of the army fell. With his death all hope was extinguished; the troops were disorganized. There was no general competent to guide them, and of course the natural sequence followed: Christians immediately found themselves subjected to a terrible persecution. A reaction set in against the Christians who had hitherto been left in comparative peace; the Muslim yoke was riveted firmer than ever, and William of Tyre (1130-1186), in his history of the war, says that it is impossible to record all the evils they suffered.

In the year 1009 Jerusalem received a greater shock than all its previous grievous experience. El Hakim (985-1021), the fanatical caliph of Egypt, invaded Palestine; the holy city was destroyed, the church covering the sacred ground was burned, but the rock of the Sepulcher resisted the fire, and the cavern of the finding was beyond its reach. The Cross was rescued by the Christians and concealed somewhere in the city. For ninety years was the holy wood hidden, ninety years of cruel suffering for the faithful, whose hearts were occasionally gladdened by a private exposition of the Tree on which their Savior experienced far greater agony, and, strengthened in this thought, they quietly bore up, true heroes, although nameless.

5

THE CRUSADES

In those regions where this persecution was made known, the anger of the faithful was aroused. At the beginning of the eleventh century, Pope Silvester II (c. 946-1003), enlightened by his own experience during a pilgrimage to Jerusalem, made an appeal to the people of north Italy and went so far as to organize an expedition of Pisans, Genoese, and the subjects of the king of Arles. They landed in Syria, but were unable to penetrate far inland; their presence, however, was not without some influence, as the persecution sensibly diminished.

Half a century later, a fresh appeal was made by Pope Gregory VII (c. 1020-1085): "The miseries suffered by the Eastern Christians," he wrote, "have so stirred up my heart that I almost long for death, and I would rather expose my life in delivering the holy places than reign over the Universe. Come, sons of Christ! And you will find me at your head." These words led fifty thousand Christians to take an oath to follow their spiritual father to Constantinople; and the emperor Michael Ducas (c. 1050-1090) promised, with their help, to replace the Crescent with the Cross.

But it all came to nothing.

RELICS FROM THE CRUCIFIXION

Henry IV (1050-1106) of Germany refused to join the expedition, and Gregory was so engrossed with the political struggles of the day that he had no time to carry out his expressed wish. His successor in the chair of St. Peter—Victor III (c. 1026-1087)—made a feeble effort in the same direction, but it was left to the next pope—Urban II (c. 1042-1099)—to give the decided word that moved so vast a multitude whose deeds altered the whole history of Europe and Western Asia.

Peter of Amiens, usually known as Peter the Hermit, was the real mover in the scheme that developed into what is known as the Crusades. He had been to the Holy Land and had seen and shared the persecution of those confessing Christ. He had wept over the desecrated places of the Crucifixion and Entombment; he had bewailed the dethronement of the Cross from its place of honor; and when praying before the Holy Sepulcher, he conceived the idea of arousing the world to rescue these places from the Saracens.

He left Palestine for Rome with letters from the Patriarch Simeon to Pope Urban, who commissioned Peter to summon the nations to a holy war. From country to country went Peter; his voice was the first to make known to the people in many regions the state of their coreligionists under Muslim rule and surprised the inhabitants of the more westerly countries whom he addressed, who imagined all things at peace in that distant country. His eloquence determined many to avenge the indignities offered to our Lord in those places consecrated by His association. The people were ripe for action, they but waited for some authorized voice to give the word of command, a voice to be listened to by all nations, a central banner around which many peoples, but of one creed, could rally, and all eyes were directed to their common spiritual father.

Thus was Urban able to accomplish that in which his two predecessors had failed.

In 1095 Urban traveled to France. He left Rome ostensibly for the support of the Gallican Church in his struggle with the anti-Pope Guibert (c. 1029-1100); but in reality, it was at the advice of Boamund (c. 1058-1111), for the purpose of inciting all Europe to undertake war to recover the holy places.

A council was held at Clermont, in Auvergne, November 18 through 28, during which decrees were confirmed and canons made. The first sittings were employed in decreeing the Truce of God between all Christians, a welding together of all the faithful; a necessary proceeding if the great proposal to follow was to be a success. At the conclusion of the preliminary business Peter the Hermit addressed the assembly with the eloquence that had already moved nations and vividly portrayed the miseries of the Church in the East.

Pope Urban then addressed the multitude on the subject so near his heart — that of driving the infidels from Palestine — with skillful and learned language:

> Go with confidence to attack the enemies of God. For they long since — oh, sad reproach to Christians! — have seized Syria, Armenia, and the provinces of Asia Minor; Bithynia, Phrygia, Galatia, Lydia, Caria, Pamphylia, Isauria, Lycia, Cilicia; and now they insolently domineer over Illyricum and all the hither countries even to the sea which is called the Straits of St. George. Nay, they usurp even the Sepulcher of our Lord, that singular assurance of our faith; and sell to our pilgrims admissions to that city which ought, had they a trace of their ancient courage left, to be open to Christians only. This alone might be

enough to cloud our brows; but now, who except the most abandoned, or the most envious of Christian reputation, can endure that we do not divide the world equally with them? They inhabit Asia, a third portion of the world, as their native soil, which was justly esteemed by our ancestors equal—by the extent of its tracts and greatness of its provinces—to the two remaining parts. There formerly sprang up the first germs of our faith; there all the Apostles except two consecrated their deaths; there at the present day the Christians, if any survive, sustaining life by a wretched kind of agriculture, pay these miscreants tribute, and even with stifled sighs long for the participation of your liberty, since they have lost their own. They hold Africa also, another quarter of the world, already possessed by their arms for more than two hundred years; which on this account I pronounce derogatory to Christian honor, because that country was anciently the nurse of celebrated geniuses, who, by their divine writings, will mock the rest of antiquity so long as there shall be one person who can appreciate Roman literature: the learned know the truth of what I say.

Let such as are going to fight for Christianity put the form of the cross upon their garments that they may outwardly demonstrate the love arising from their inward faith, enjoying by the gift of God and the privilege of St. Peter, absolution from all their sins. Let this in the meantime soothe the labor of their journey, satisfied that they shall obtain after death the advantages of a blessed martyrdom. Putting, then, an end to your crimes, that Christians at least may live peaceably in these countries, go, and employ in nobler warfare that valor, and that sagacity, which you used to waste in civil broils. Go, soldiers, everywhere renowned in fame, go and subdue these dastardly nations.[7]

These extracts from Pope Urban's inspiriting address to the French people give us an insight into the origin of the spirit that inflamed all Europe, that led to great aspirations, many noble deeds, and, alas, much bloodshed and personal animosity.

The majority of the pope's audience, fired with enthusiasm by his eloquence, attested their eagerness in the cause by rising in a body, and one prolonged shout burst forth simultaneously, "*Dieu le veut*" (God wills it). *Dieu le veut*, words for two centuries destined to be the war cry of those soldiers of the Cross. Immediately, in the presence of the council, many of the nobility consecrated themselves and their property to the service of God.

"Let the cross," said Urban, "glitter on your arms and on your standards. Bear it on your shoulders and on your breasts. It will become for you the emblem of victory or the palm of martyrdom; it will ever remind you that Jesus Christ died for you, and that it is your part to die for Him."

The movement, begun here, soon spread throughout Christian countries. To regain Jerusalem was the all-absorbing topic. To such an extent were people carried away with the idea that it led to whole families migrating. "The rustic," says Guibert of Nogent (1055-1124), "shod his oxen like horses, and placed all his family on a cart; where it was amusing to hear the children, as they approached any large town or castle, asking if that was Jerusalem." The number to assume the Cross is estimated by

---

[7] William of Malmesbury, *Deeds of the English Kings* (1095), 4:2.

Fulcher of Chartres (1059-c. 1128) to have been six million. Never before did so many nations unite for one object.

In the spring of 1096 departed the first Crusaders in two great bodies, under the leadership of Peter the Hermit and Gautier Sans-Avoir (d. 1096). These undisciplined masses, without means, supported themselves on the road by pillage. This, of course, was resented by the nations through whose territories they passed, and who, in their wrath, dispersed and almost annihilated them. The remnant reached Constantinople in a pitiable condition, where they were succored by the Emperor Alexius I (1056-1118) and where they awaited the arrival of the troops that had started three months later under Godfrey de Bouillon.

The entire history of the First, Second, and part of the Third Crusade belongs to the history of the Cross; yet they cannot be dwelt upon here except so far as they directly affect that history.

Godfrey de Bouillon, Duke of Lorraine, whose generalship was acknowledged as preeminent, led the Frisons, Lorrainers, Saxons, and all the people who dwelt between the Rhine and the Elbe, by way of Hungary. Raimund, Earl of St. Giles and Aimar (d. 1098), the warlike bishop of Puy, led the Goths, the Gascons, and the inhabitants of the Pyrenees and the Alps, through Dalmatia. Boamund, with the Italians of the various states, went by sea from Brindisi to Durazzo. Robert of Flanders, followed by the English, Flemish, Normans, and Western Franks, went by way of Lucca. And so these different sections of a vast host pressed forward with one noble intent, but accompanied with pitiable circumstances unavoidable in an unorganized multitude. Want and exposure thinned the ranks of many; and the utter ignorance of the distance of their goal led numbers of the peasantry to abandon the enterprise when they found what privations had to be encountered. Extreme poverty, encumbered with large families

Fig. 5: Statue of Godfrey de Bouillon.

in many cases, and in a foreign land: no wonder the simple folks became disheartened and gave up that which their presence could only hinder.

It is not, however, our province to follow the Crusaders in their varying fortunes, their feats of arms, or their tactical blunders, until Jerusalem was rescued.

It was the sixth of June, 1099, when the Crusaders arrived before the walls of the Holy City, but between fighting the infidels and quarelling among themselves, the Christians were making little real progress. While things were in this state, Adhemar

(d. 1098), bishop of Puy, is said to have appeared to Peter the Hermit and promised that the city of Jerusalem would fall if the Christian host encompassed it, barefoot, for nine days. Humility, a virtue sadly lacking in their breasts, was necessary to the success of a holy undertaking. A general reconciliation took place, and, while not neglecting militant matters, the ghostly injunctions of Adhemar were observed.

Following the bishops and clergy, the whole army, with bare feet, slowly marched in one great procession around the walls. The Saracens clustered on the ramparts to watch such novel proceedings, and mocked them in derision; to do this more effectually they brought the Holy Cross on to the walls and while beating it, they shouted, "Franks, this is the blessed cross." No action was more calculated to reunite the divided warriors.

On Friday morning, July 13, the Christian army regained Jerusalem.

The carnage was fearful. The excited Crusaders had been wrought to a state of fanaticism. They spared no one; the chivalrous arm forgot sex and age; in the women they saw only infidels who had profaned the Cross and defiled those places sacred to their Lord; in the children they saw but the evil spawn of the desecrators. The air was rent with the awful sound of battle, shouts of defiance and of triumph, the hideous sound of shrill wailings of the women, heard only in the countries of the East; but above all this noise of Satanic cabal there arose a sound from the very heart of the city. It was not loud, but it thrilled through every heart of those fierce Western warriors, who seemed suddenly calmed by an invisible spell. The carnage ceased, a sudden stillness took possession of the city, and the weapons fell from the grasp of the soldiers, as with unutterable joy they gazed in an ecstasy toward a procession of priests. Then, as with one accord, all knees were bent in adoration, for there was the wood on which their Lord had poured out His blood for them. The True Cross was being borne through their midst.

For ninety years it had remained in the custody of the bishops of Jerusalem, concealed from the Saracens, who wondered at the mysterious power it exercised over their enemies, and feared its presence more than the combined armies of the West. Only in the tumult caused by the appearance of the Crusaders around the walls, in confidence of a speedy delivery, had the custodians of that relic revealed its asylum. Once again had the Cross been seized by the infidel—with the intention of desecration—at the crucial moment for the revival of the waning zeal of the Christian army. The means adopted by the followers of a false prophet had been overruled to defeat their ends.

Now that once again it was among them, joyfully the chant of *Benedicite* rose loud and clear as the procession passed through the host, headed by Daimbert (d. 1105), the legate, bearing the sacred wood over the bloodstained path. The infidels felt how complete their enemies' victory was and died with impotent curses lingering on their lips. The dying Crusaders made one effort to behold it through their dimming eyes and sank back to yield their souls in peace. Many were the lips that murmured *Nunc dimittis* on that memorable Friday.

Bareheaded and unarmed, closely following the Cross came Godfrey, Tancred, Raimund, and many others whose names will live through all time as champions of Christendom. Never was victory more intensely appreciated than that which saved the wood of the Cross from ignominy and replaced it on Calvary.

Godfrey was elected the first king by the leaders of the combined armies, under the modest title of "Baron of the Holy Sepulcher," and thus was founded the Kingdom of Jerusalem, which lasted eighty-seven years. As the kings of the Holy City died, they were laid to rest at the foot of that wood that it had been their one aim to protect. Godfrey slept on the right of it, Baldwin I (1058-1118) on the left.

We hear of the Holy Cross being borne in battle and leading to victory the Christian troops when Baldwin led his 240 knights and 900 foot soldiers, on September the 7, 1101, to conquer the infidel hosts to the number of 11,000 horse and 21,000 foot soldiers, near the town of Jaffa; as also Euremar, the archbishop of Caesarea, had the same honor at the relief of Antioch on August 14, 1119, when he elevated it in the face of the enemy and in its name solemnly cursed them.

The youthful Baldwin III (1130-1163), when he met with a reverse on the plain of Medan, near Tiberias, in 1145, was urged by the barons to mount a fleet horse and with the Cross to flee to a place of safety; but he scorned so unworthy an act and would not withdraw the inspiring presence of the Cross at the moment that it was the means of diverting despair. The Christians made an orderly retreat, but when the smoke from the thickets, fired by the Saracens, was blown into their faces, their condition became almost intolerable. The soldiers raised their smoke-begrimed faces to the Holy Cross. "Pray for us" they cried, feeling in a state beyond hope. Robert, archbishop of Nazareth, who bore the Cross on this occasion, advanced toward the flames with it held aloft; as he did so, they seemed to retreat, the wind changed its course, and the Christians gained the field of Gadara.

The Cross is said to have been carried to the gate of the city when Baldwin went to meet the Saracens at Askelon, and again in that battle, victorious for the faithful, it was actually in the field; though some are of the opinion that it never left its shrine until that fatal day at Hattin, when Guy of Lusignan (1150-1194), the last of the kings, lost the Kingdom of Jerusalem.

And where was the spot so honored by its presence?

A few paces to the east of the Sepulcher was the rock of Calvary, there the wood of the Cross was enshrined, and as the pilgrims entered, they knelt first at the Cross and then at the tomb.

In all the history of Christendom, no scene is found more profoundly sad than when Guy, the king of Jerusalem, called his knights to hold council in the camp at Sephouri, July 1, 1187, when engaged in the last struggle with Saladin. The leaders and motives of former days had passed away, Godfrey and Baldwin were lying at the foot of Calvary, a fitting spot for such men; but with them the use of arms for high ideals had gone also, and weapons were now become merely the means to minister to the lusts of greed and ambition. Yet not all: some few characters shone forth with the bright luster of the old Faith, and bitter was their grief that inward dissensions should have eclipsed the Faith for which they fought.

Raymond III (1140-1187), count of Tripoli, tore himself away from his own beleaguered city of Tiberias by the Sea of Galilee, where his lady was surrounded by the Saracens, to join the army at Sephouri under his old enemy Guy. The terrible importance of the Christian cause at this time marked the path of duty to Raymond. Sinking personal enmity and family ties, he brought his sword to Guy's banner, only to find that the Grand Master of the Templars and other knights were jealous of his presence and opposed his councils. The question before them was whether they should cross the burning plain, attack the Saracens and relieve Tiberias or permit the fall of that stronghold and await a more favorable opportunity for the decisive battle. Raymond, whose personal interests were in Tiberias, counseled the latter course, for, said he, his castle could be regained and his wife rescued from captivity, but the defeat of this army would mean the loss of the whole kingdom. The temper of the knights grew hot; the Grand Master of the Templars boldly charged Raymond with treason and denounced his policy. King Guy was persuaded, against his better judgment, to ignore Count Raymond and to lead his army to Tiberias.

The hostile armies were encamped within a few miles of each other. In the center of the Christian camp was the wood of the Cross that Guy had persuaded the patriarch to send from Jerusalem to Galilee to revive the declining courage of the troops. It was sent in charge of the bishop of Ptolemais (Acre) and the bishop of St. George (Lydda). It was, however, looked upon only by a people undeserving the name of their ancestors, with a superstitious hope that it might prove a charm and without that reverence for Him who thereon bled for their salvation, which had been the inspiration of their predecessors.

Opposed to Guy, who was an exceptional disgrace to Christianity, was Saladin—an exceptional glory to Mohammedanism. The acts of the latter are a pleasure to dwell upon.

Yielding to the advice of the Grand Master, Guy moved his army out into the plain of Hattin, and the sultan advanced to meet him. Then was the counsel of Raymond remembered. The heat was terrible, there was no water, and the knights were fainting in their heavy armor. The Saracens held all the positions of importance when the battle commenced on the fourth of July, a day of fearful carnage, and when night fell, it left the field undecided. The morning following, the heat was yet worse, and the Saracens, taking advantage of the wind that was blowing in the direction of the European camp, set fire to the grass; the plain became a veritable furnace. Then once again, although too late, knight and Templar forgot their differences and shoulder to shoulder vied with each other in defending the Cross.

Saladin observed the wonderful inspiring power of this beam of wood and directed his strongest forces to its capture. He remarked that the Franks rallied around it with the utmost bravery "as if they believed it their greatest blessing, strongest band of union, and surest defense." As the day wore on, the hosts of the Saracens closed in on the diminishing numbers of the Christians, until the fight was concentrated around a slight eminence on which was upheld the Cross. No one thought of the king: the eyes of the doomed again saw their Savior stretched on that wood for them and devotedly laid down their lives for its attempted preservation from desecration. The last man fell, and the Cross was held by the conquerors. Who that last man was no one knows; but he fell, surrounded by the bodies of those who had fought for that same object, crushing with mace or hewing with two-edged sword the heads of the crowding infidels.

That beam of the Cross was lost on July 5, 1187, never again to come into the possession of Christians. His army rejoiced over the coveted riches of the shrine, but Saladin's joy was that he had taken from his enemies that piece of old wood that had proved such an incentive to their energy and that, strange as it appeared to him, they prized far beyond all the gold and jewels.

The victory was complete: king and Templars, the Christian army and their treasure had been taken. Once again the noble character of Saladin, the enemy of our Faith, stands in bold relief from the surroundings of that age. He liberated those who were simply pilgrims; yielded seven hundred captives to the patriarch who applied to him; and gave liberty to all those who were too poor to pay the ransom of ten dinors a man, five for a woman, and two for a child.

RELICS FROM THE CRUCIFIXION

Such beneficence was emulated by his brother, Seif ed-Din, who said to Saladin and besought him thus: "I have fought well; give me one thousand slaves." This was done, and they were immediately set free. He then gave from his treasury to the widows and orphans of the Christian knights who had fallen in battle; he sent troops with them as they went to that part of the land yet in their possession, that they might assist the wounded and the feeble; and those soldiers, whom we are apt to consider barbarians, were so imbued with the chivalric spirit that became so famous in the West that they put the women on their horses, walking with the children in their arms—a truly noble treatment of the vanquished.

With the capitulation of Jerusalem shortly afterward (October 2) ended the kingdom founded by Godfrey. Christendom was in mourning. All Europe rang with grief when it was known that the Cross was lost.

An attempt was soon after made by certain Christians to throw discredit on the wood in the possession of the Saracens. A Knight Templar declared to Henry of Champagne (1166-1197) that during the battle he had buried the Cross on the field and marked the spot, while that seized by Saladin was a piece of wood substituted for the actual relic. When a search was made, however, nothing was found, and there is no doubt it was in the sultan's hands.

Repeated efforts were made by King Richard of England (1157-1199) between the years 1190 and 1192 to purchase the Cross from Saladin, who refused at any price to restore to his foes that which infused such vigor into their arms.

At the siege of Acre in 1190 the Sultan agreed to restore it on certain conditions. On Friday after the feast of the Translation of the Relics of St. Benedict, 1191, hostages were exchanged, and the space of one month fixed for the delivery of the Cross. At the expiration of the month, Saladin failed to keep to the terms of the treaty; he asked for a longer time to make a search for it. It was a time of suppressed excitement among the Christians. Rumors spread that it was coming into the camp, then that it was totally lost, or that it had been seen in the camp of the Saracens. The fact was, says Geoffrey de Vinsauf (c. 1200), that Saladin had taken no steps to restore the Cross, hoping to obtain more advantageous terms.

During the years 1191 to 1192 we occasionally hear of it as being kept in Jerusalem by the sultan, who allowed some of the English pilgrims to see and kiss it; among them was Hubert Walter (c. 1160-1205), the bishop of Salisbury, who obtained permission for two Latin priests to conduct services in the Church of the Holy Sepulchre.

Since then it is known no more. The great portion of the Cross for which so much blood was spilled is suddenly lost to history. Saladin either hid or destroyed that talisman whose invisible power he could not understand; and now it probably forms part of the soil of Palestine; or it was burned (as reported) and the dust wafted by the winds over the face of the globe to sanctify the whole earth.

In its earlier history, some portion of the Cross must have been carried to Antioch as, at the burning of that city by Chosroes, the bishop of Apamea consented to expose it for the adoration of the faithful, and that their last kiss of the sacred relic might be, as it were, their viaticum to Paradise. This is related by Evagrius (b. c. 536), who says that he was present and describes the scene at some length, telling us how the bishop, while making the circuit of the church, carrying the Cross, was followed by a huge mass of flame, blazing but not consuming, a token of the safety vouchsafed to the city.

RELICS FROM THE CRUCIFIXION

When Richard I was at Betenople, on his way to Jerusalem, he had brought to him, according to Geoffrey de Vinsauf, two pieces of the Cross: one by the Syrian bishop of St. George, who came accompanied by a large concourse of people, with his present of the holy wood, hailing him as their deliverer. The other he obtained through the venerable abbot of St. Elie, who came to the king on St. Alban's day, 1192, to tell him that he had a long time ago concealed a piece of the Holy Cross in order to preserve it until the Holy Land should be rescued from the infidels and that he alone knew of this hidden treasure. He had often been hard pressed by Saladin, who had tried to make him reveal the hiding place by the most searching inquiries. He had, however, always baffled his interrogators by ambiguous replies and deluded them with false statements, and on account of his contumacy Saladin had ordered him to be bound, but he, persisting in asserting that he had lost it during the taking of Jerusalem, was allowed to go free. The king at once set out with the abbot and a number of followers to the place where it had been buried, and having taken up the piece of the Holy Cross with humble veneration, they bore it into camp amid the rejoicings of the army. That it was a piece of the True Cross seems to have been taken for granted with no further evidence than that of the abbot.

Perhaps it was one of these two pieces that King Richard gave to the patriarch when at Jerusalem—a piece that passed into the possession of the archbishop of Cyprus, who publicly presented it as a national offering to Sir Sidney Smith (1764-1840) "in the name of a grateful people." Sir Sidney Smith bequeathed it to the Convent of the Order of St. John of Jerusalem, at Paris, as being the successors of the Templars.

Surely the greatest price ever given for a fragment of the True Cross and that with no exchange of money, was paid by a

Norwegian king, Sigurd (c. 1090-1130), known in the sagas as "the Crusader." At the age of eighteen, following the example of his race, Sigurd left Norway at the head of ten thousand warriors to seek fame in distant lands. He sailed through the Straits of Gibraltar, and for a year distinguished himself by deeds of valor in fighting the Moors of Spain and Morocco.

Arrived at Palestine, he made his pilgrimage to the shrine of the Cross in Jerusalem and requested a relic of the holy wood. King Baldwin I was at that time in want of naval assistance for the reduction of Sidon, and he made an agreement with Sigurd that, if he would help in the siege of Sidon, at that time the strongest port in the land, when it capitulated he should receive a piece of the Cross as his sole reward, and relinquish all rights of conquest to Baldwin.

Sidon fell, and the saga of Sigurd relates how King Baldwin and the patriarch caused a splinter of the wood to be taken off the Cross, and on it "they both made oath that this wood was of the Holy Cross upon which God Himself had been tortured." Then was this holy relic given to Prince Sigurd, with the condition that he and twelve other men with him should swear to promote Christianity with all their power and erect an archbishop's seat in Norway; that the Cross should be kept where the holy King Olaf was buried; and also that he should introduce tithes and pay them himself.

Sigurd in time became sole king of Norway, and he built the "Cross Church" in his castle of Konghelle, where he deposited the piece of the Cross in 1127.

A morsel of this relic found its way into Denmark and was enclosed in a reliquary cross of the good Queen Dagmar (1186-1212). At her death in 1212, it was laid upon her breast and buried with her. In after ages, her tomb was opened, and the

Fig. 6: Dagmar Cross containing a relic of the True Cross.

relic, which was taken out, is now in the Museum at Copen-hagen. The jewel is of Byzantine workmanship and enameled with icons of Christ, the Blessed Virgin, St. John, St. Basil, and St. Chrysostom.

The other large piece of the Cross, which was deposited in Constantinople, has a yet more indefinite history than that which was preserved in Jerusalem. It would seem to have been subdivided to an even greater extent, and what with giving, sell-ing, and stealing, but little can be traced.

In writing of this piece of the Cross, Socrates Scholasticus (c. 380-439) tells us that Constantine, being persuaded that the city would be rendered impregnable where that relic should be preserved, privately enclosed a piece of it in his own statue, which stood on a large column of porphyry in the forum called Constantine. This colossal bronze statue is said to have formerly represented Apollo and was transferred from Athens, or from some town of Phrygia, and appropriated by the emperor to himself, being afterward known as that of Constantine the Great. It was one of the sights of Constantinople as late as the fifteenth century.

We obtain further information of that wood of the Cross that was enshrined at Constantinople from the writings of the literary emperor Constantine Porphyrogenitus (905-959), in the middle of the tenth century, whose pen has been the means of revealing much that is known of the Byzantine Empire.

In *De ceremoniis Aulae Byzantinae*, he says that it was the custom, about seven days before the first of August, for the Holy Cross to be taken out of the sacred treasury in which it was kept with other precious relics and rich holy vessels, between the third and sixth ode of Matins. It was laid on the ground so that the *protopapa*, or chief priest of the palace, might anoint it all over with balsam and precious perfumes. Then it was set up in the Church of the Palace of Our Lady of the Pharos and exposed to the veneration of the people. After Matins, the clergy of the palace assembled before it, singing praise of the Cross in hymns called *Staurosima*. Then the princes and nobles came to venerate it before they assisted at the Sunday's procession, in which they accompanied the emperor — every Sunday and holy day — to the divine service in the church of the palace, or on certain great festivals to one of the principal churches in the city. The protopapa, having on a purple cassock and over it a rich *scaramangium* (a large vesture that covers the whole body) and attended by the clergy and others, took up the Cross and carried it in procession on the top of his head through the Golden Hall and placed it before the oratory of St. Basil, to be venerated by all the senate. He then proceeded to the Palace of Daphne and exposed it in the Church of St. Stephen. On the twenty-eighth of July, the priests began to carry the Cross through all the streets and to all the houses and then around the walls of the city, that by the devotion of the people and their united prayers, God would, through the Cross and merits of His Son, bless and protect the city and all its inhabitants.

On the thirteenth of September (the vigil of the Greek combined feasts of the Finding and the Exaltation), it was brought back to the palace and placed on a rich throne in the Chrysotriclinium, or Golden Hall, where the clergy sang the hymns in praise of the Cross during its exaltation there. It was afterward carried through all the apartments of the palace and deposited in the chapel of St. Theodorus. In the evening it was delivered back to the keeper of the sacred treasury. Next morning it was carefully cleansed by the protopapa and the custodian and again deposited in the rich shrine in the treasury.

Out of the holy wood that was brought to Constantinople, three crosses must have been fashioned, for we again read in the eleventh chapter of the emperor's work:

> With what devotion and pomp the three large crosses kept in the great palace were taken out in the third or middle week of Lent, and exposed to veneration, one in the new church of this great palace, another in the Church of St. Stephen in the palace of Daphne, and the third in the patriarchal Church of St. Sophia. All the three crosses were again brought back on Friday in the same week in solemn procession with torches and singing.

After Baldwin I, the first of the Latin emperors of Constantinople, was defeated by the Bulgarians — about 1205 — in which engagement he failed to carry the Cross with the army, one of his chaplains, an Englishman, hearing the emperor was killed, is said to have left the city privately with some of the relics. Arrived in England, he tried to sell the Cross to the monks of St. Alban's, but as he had no proofs of authenticity, they refused to credit his story, and he departed, going to one after another of the greater monasteries, only to be repulsed. He at length reached the Cluniac Priory of St. Andrew at Bromeholme, in Norfolk, a small and poverty-stricken house. There he showed to the prior and some of the brethren the relics in his possession, among them the cross he professed to have brought from Constantinople and begged that he might be received into their community, together with these treasures. The prior received him on these terms, and, with great reverence, carried the cross into their oratory, where it was enshrined in the most honorable place.

It is said that miracles immediately began to take place; and the fame of it rapidly spread, not only in the British Isles but over a great part of Europe; and among the pilgrims who came to adore it were many noble foreigners.

This relic was composed of two pieces of wood placed across one another and was almost as wide as a man's hand.

Henry III (1207-1272) granted to the monks of Bromeholme Priory the privilege of an annual fair on the festival of the Exaltation of the Holy Cross, on account of the honor of possessing such a relic.

The Cross of Cnerth, Neet, or Neyth was obtained by the king in 1283 at the conquest of Wales, as a part of the True Cross, it had been taken to that country by St. Neot (d. c. 870), who had received it from King Alfred (849-899).

Of all the countries possessing particles of this precious relic, Mount Athos has more than any other one place.

6

LITERATURE ON THE CROSS

The love of the Cross has inspired poets and has created abundant literature on that subject; it has burst forth into hymns of praise that will last through all the ages and shine forth with supreme luster amid the exuberance of modern hymnology. The prose and poetry of our Saxon forefathers on this subject is extensive, yet largely unknown.

In whatever spirit the story of the Cross may be received, whether or not it was the very cross of our Savior that St. Helena found, it must be thankfully acknowledged that to it we owe the valued heritage of our most beautiful compositions. Some of these songs of praise have stirred Christendom for more than thirteen hundred years, sanctified by their venerable use as well as by the origin of their inspiration.

The "Pange Lingua" ("Sing my tongue, the Savior's glory") which year by year is raised by innumerable voices, is a passionate eulogy on the Cross, written by Venantius Fortunatus (c. 530-c. 605), from whom we also have the inspiring song "Vexilla Regis"—"The Royal Banners Forward Go"—composed about the year 580. The latter was written for a procession at the consecration of a church at Poitiers by St. Gregory of Tours, who had received a piece of the True Cross among other relics to deposit in that sanctuary.

In 847 Rhaban Maur (780-856), archbishop of Mainz, wrote a poem in honor of the Cross; and countless poets have taken the Holy Cross for their theme, some of their compositions being introduced into the Liturgy proper for the special festivals of the Holy Cross.

In the *Paracletice* (or *Great Octoechus*) of the Greek Church, a book containing the Ferial Office for eight weeks, in which most of the hymns are written by St. Joseph of the Studium, is a Canon of the Cross for every Sunday and Wednesday.

The following sequence for the Finding of the Holy Cross — "Salve, crux sancta" — is in the *Sarum Missal* and is a translation by C. B. Pearson:

Thou holy Cross, all hail!
Thou tree of dignity!
The costly price at which the world
Was prized once hung on thee.

That so the ancient foe
Who triumphed by a tree,
Should by a Tree discomforted
Lose all his victory.

And what brought death to man
Cast out of Paradise,
Might be the cause of life to all
Who by Christ's death arise.

A spectacle of dread
To our fell enemies

Ever thou art, O holy Cross,
Scaring their evil eyes.

That which strikes death with awe
And hell with dire dismay
His own doth seal for Christ anew:
To whom be praise for aye.

The hymn of Adam of St. Victor (d. 1146) — "Laudes Crucis attollamus" — was used as a sequence on the feast of the Exaltation of the Holy Cross by the Church of Sarum:

Let us extol the Cross's praise,
And in its special glory raise
Exultingly our voice;

For by the Cross we triumph gain,
And o'er the cruel foe obtain
Life-giving victory.

Let dulcet sound to heaven resound,
O'er the sweet wood of holy Rood
Rejoice, as it is meet.
Let life and words concordant be:
When life at one with words we see,
The symphony is sweet.

The Cross let all its servants praise,
By which new life and healthful days
Upon them are bestowed;

Let each and all together cry,
Hail, Cross! The world's recovery,
Salvation-bearing Rood!

RELICS FROM THE CRUCIFIXION

O how blessèd, how renowned
Is this saving Altar found
   On which the Lamb was slain;
Spotless Lamb, by whom mankind
Full deliverance doth find
   From sin's primeval stain.

The ladder this to sinners given,
By means of which Christ, King of heaven,
   Drew to Him all our race;
This doth the form thereof display —
The arms, outstretching every way
   The world's four parts embrace.

These are not novel mysteries,
Not newly doth the Cross uprise
   Its mighty power to show;
This sweetened erst the bitter well
Moses did from the rock compel
   Water by this to flow.

No safety in the house abides
Till by the Cross who there resides
   His threshold doth secure.
No danger from the murderous foe,
No sad bereavement doth he know,
   Who thus doth help procure.

The widow, lacking fire and food,
Who at Sarepta gathered wood,
   The hope of safety gained;
Without two sticks for faith to use,
Barrel of meal and scanty cruse

Literature on the Cross

Had increase ne'er obtained.

In ancient writ the Cross lay hid,
Yet types did show what now we know;
    To us 'tis brought to light.
Kings credence give, foes cease to strive;
By this alone, Christ leading, one
    Doth thousands put to flight.

The Cross doth make its servants brave,
And every victory to have;
Heals weakness and diseases grave;
    Before it devils cower.

This to the captive freedom gives,
Regenerates our vicious lives,
All ancient dignity revives
    Beneath the Cross's power.

O holy Cross, triumphant Tree
The world's true health, all hail to thee!
Amidst the trees none such can be
    In leaf, or flower, or bud.

Medicine of the Christian soul,
Heal thou the sick, preserve the whole;
Things which no mortal can control
    Cannot thy power elude.

Those who the Cross didst hallow, hear
Us who that holy Cross revere;
The servants of Thy Cross convey
Unto the realms of changeless day,
    When this life's toils are o'er.

RELICS FROM THE CRUCIFIXION

Those whom by pain Thou makest pure
From everlasting pains secure
And when the Day of Wrath shall come,
Of thy vast mercy fetch us home
To joys for evermore.

Our own countrymen were not inferior to those authors already mentioned in contributing to the literature on the Cross. Although the style of our Teutonic forefathers may be somewhat heavier than their Latin contemporaries, their compositions breathe fully as much of fervor for the Faith and of poetical imagination. The early Northern scald's mode of expression will be more fully appreciated when the modern reader is more conversant with their writings.

A volume of Saxon manuscripts containing two poems on the Holy Cross was found at Vercelli, in north Italy. One is a "Dream of the Holy Rood," and the other is about the finding of the Cross by the empress Helena.

In the "Dream" the dreamer saw the Cross as if it were a beacon, so brilliantly did it gleam with gold and gems, yet through the gold he beheld bloodstained wood, and as he gazed he heard the holy wood speak:

'Twas many a year ago,
I yet remember it,
that I was hewn down
at the woods' end,
cut from my stem.

Strong foes took me thence;
they made me for a spectacle;
they bade me uplift their outcasts;
there men bore me upon their shoulders

until they set me down upon a hill,
there foes enough fastened me.

There saw I the Lord of mankind
hasten with mighty power,
because he would mount on me.

There I then dared not,
against the Lord's command,
bow down or burst asunder;
though I saw tremble
the whole of the earth.

I had power all
his foes to fell,
but yet I stood fast.

Then the young hero prepared himself —
that was Almighty God,
strong and firm of will.

He mounted the lofty cross
brave in the sight of many,
when he willed to redeem mankind.

I trembled when the hero embraced me,
yet dared I not bow down to earth
or fall to the bosom of the ground,
but I was compelled to stand fast.

A cross was I reared,
I raised the great King,
the Lord of the heavens,
yet dared I not stoop.

RELICS FROM THE CRUCIFIXION

They pierced me with dark nails
on me are the wounds visible,
open witnesses of mischief:
I dared not harm any of them.

They reviled us both together.

I was all stained with blood
that poured from His side
when He as man
His spirit sent on its way.

Many a bitter pang I endured
there upon that mount;
I saw the Lord of Hosts cruelly beset;

Darkness had
concealed with clouds
the Ruler's corpse,
the clear brightness.

The shadow went forth,
wan 'neath the welkin.

All creation wept,
they mourned the fall of their King;
Christ was on the Cross.

Then thither hastening
came men from afar
unto the noble One.

All this I saw,
With sorrow I was overwhelmed.

I bowed to the hands of men humbly
with all my strength.

Then took they thence Almighty God
and raised him from the wood.

The warriors left me there
standing stained all with blood;
I was wounded with shafts.

They laid him down limb-weary;
they stood by His head;
they beheld the Lord of heaven,
and there awhile He rested
weary after His mighty contest.

We, crosses, awhile stood there
in our place, weeping;
until fierce warriors came
and felled us to the earth, and
in a deep pit hid us.

But me the servants of the Lord there found;
with silver and with gold
they decked me o'er.

This manuscript, which is of the early part of the eleventh century and is in the Wessex dialect, has been transcribed from an earlier original by a certain Cynewulf. It is a copy of a far older poem, for on the Ruthwell Cross, in Northumbrian Runic characters, are portions of this very poem, with runes saying, "Caedmon made me." Whether this refers to the poem or to the stone cross, it brings it to about the same date—the end of the seventh century—and we possibly have here the visionary poetry of our own native poet, Caedmon the herdsman (d. c. 680), inspired by the accounts of the Exaltation of the Holy Cross some fifty years before.

The source of the poem on the finding of the Cross in the *Vercelli Codex* is evidently the Latin *Life of Cyriacus*, which is printed in the *Acta Sanctorum* for the fifth of May; and that is probably translated from a yet earlier Greek original. The mode of treating this subject by our Saxon poet is, however, worthy of a wider acquaintance.

The vision of Constantine, while encamped on the battlefield, which is said to have revealed to him the irresistible power that should lead him to victory, is thus described:

> *To him appeared, beauteous*
> *in the form of man*
> *white and bright of hue,*
> *I know not what hero*
> *revealed, more fair*
> *than he before or since*
> *had seen beneath the firmament:*
> *he woke up from sleep*
> *covered with his boar-shaped helm.*
>
> *Him soon the messenger,*
> *the bright messenger of glory,*
> *addressed,*
> *and named him by his name,*
> *the helm of night departed:*
>
> *"Constantinus,*
> *to thee the king of angels bids me*
> *the wielder of fate,*

his covenant offer,
the lord of dignities;
dread not thou
though thee the strangers
terribly threaten
with hard war.

Look thou to heaven
on the ward of glory,
there shalt thou find my track
token of triumph."

He was soon ready
by the holy one's command;
he opened his thought-locks;
he looked up
as the messenger commanded him,
the gentle weaver of peace.

He saw, bright with ornaments
the beauteous tree of glory
above the roof of heaven
adorned with gold;
the gems lightened.

The pale beam
was inscribed with letters,
bright and light:

"With this sign thou
in the fierce journey
thy foe shall overcome,
shalt stop the hostile force."

RELICS FROM THE CRUCIFIXION

Then vanished the light,
up it departed,
and with it the messenger
into the company of the pure.

The king was the blither
and the freer from sorrow,
prince of men,
in his mind,
through the fair vision.

In the same Saxon poem is described the conversion of a Jewish man and his digging for the Cross by Helena's direction:

Then began he well pleased
after the tree of glory,
intent on power,
the earth to delve
under the circuit of turf,
until he twenty
foot measures deep
found it concealed,
low beneath the downward
promontory hidden
in chests of darkness.

There found he three
in the dank dwelling
crosses together,
buried in the sand.

To her the ruler of spirits

spake from heaven,
and commanded the cross itself
with gold to work up
and with kind of gems,
with the noblest jewels
to set with art,
and it in a silver vessel
with locks to shut,
wherein the tree of life
best of victorious beams
since hath remained,
a noble fragment.

The two last extracts reveal the nature of the reports and the description of the place where the Cross was found, which were current in England. They would be related and spread by the returned pilgrims and later by the warriors. The description of the cavern in which the crosses were discovered as "a deep pit" and "in chests of darkness" are verified by the present knowledge of that place.

THE SUPERSCRIPTION

The Greek τίτλοS, the Latin equivalent of which is *titulus*, primarily signifies "to hold up or out," that is, to notify something connected with it. Here it is applied to the board with the inscription fixed up to announce publicly the cause of condemnation. It is an oriental custom of great antiquity to affix these τίτλοι above every malefactor about to be executed. It is still observed in parts of Turkey and in countries further east. Josephus (37-c.100) tells us that it was usual at the time of Christ's Crucifixion to set up public notices in different languages. As everyone understood one or another of the three tongues, it was thus made legible to all.

Above our Lord's head, as He hung upon the Cross, was nailed an inscription declaring His royal title, a derisive title, in reference to the victim: a mocking title, leveled at the Jews by the Roman governor; yet through that sarcasm was a deeper meaning. It was a conviction, though undefined, that in some way it was their king for whose blood the Jews clamored, which prompted Pilate to dictate the inscription—Jesus of Nazareth, King of the Jews—and to answer the protest of the chief priests, "What I have written I have written" (John 19:22). The opposition of the priests availed nothing, nor was the declaration to be confined to the Hebrews: it was also written in Greek and Latin.

The tablet is generally said to have been found by St. Helena separate but near the Cross. Sts. Ambrose and Chrysostom, however, agree in stating that it was still adhering to the Cross when discovered. This inscription, together with some pieces of the Cross, was sent by St. Helena to Rome, where a basilica was built in which to preserve it.

Rome's Church of Santa Croce in Jerusalemme is said by some to have been founded by Constantine; by others it is attributed to St. Helena; but all declare that the foundations were laid in earth brought from Jerusalem. Severano (c. 1630) states that the tablet was originally deposited in the church by the emperor Valentinian.

The superscription was enclosed in a leaden casket and walled up in a niche above the vaulted roof of the church, and an inscription in mosaic was carved into the wall that shielded it.

As ages passed, the Church of Santa Croce was neglected, the mosaic lettering became illegible, and the holy wood was forgotten, until at length it was only by tradition that the sacred relic had any connection with the church. It was known not to be among the treasures in the sacristy, and the closed niche was never dreamed of.

On February 1, 1492, during the restoration of the church by Cardinal Mendozza, the workmen broke through the partition into the recess, where they found a leaden box "two palms long, and well fastened." Thinking that they had found a treasure, they concealed it until they could privately open it and the expected riches could be appropriated by them; but when they found in it only a piece of rotten and musty wood, they handed over to the authorities what was indeed a treasure invaluable.

On the marble of the niche above the box was the writing, "*Hic est titulus S. Crucis.*" Within the casket was found a piece of wood "a palm and a half long, and a palm wide," decayed and crumbling, especially on one side. The letters of the inscription had been incised and colored red, but the two last letters of the word *Judaeorum*, in the Latin, IESVS NAZARENVS REX IVDAE-ORVM, had rotted away.

Each of the four Evangelists gives a slightly different reading of the inscription:

St. Matthew: "This is Jesus the King of the Jews."

St. Mark: "The King of the Jews."

St. Luke: "This is the King of the Jews."

St. John: "Jesus of Nazareth, the King of the Jews."

The remains of the reading on the tablet and St. John's record are the same. That beloved disciple had stood by his King and Savior through that agony, and as he gazed on that dying face the superscription must have been indelibly graven on his brain. In another particular, St. John's description verifies the fragment left to us; the arrangement of the several languages. The first line is in Hebrew, the second in Greek, and the last in Latin. St. Luke says Greek, Latin, and Hebrew; while the other two Evangelists are quiet on this point.

Rome's joy at finding itself the possessor of such a priceless relic was beyond all description. The inscription set above the head of our Lord by a Roman governor in derision became an object of adoration in that pagan's own city of Rome. Pope Alexander VI (1431-1503) mentions this discovery in the bull *Admirabile Sacramentum* in 1496 and in it concedes an indulgence to the Church of Santa Croce on the anniversaries of this second finding.

Arnold von Harff (1471-1505) visited Rome in 1497, five years after the discovery, noting that "above an archway, in a hole in the wall, lies part of the title of Jesus Christ which Pilate wrote."

Severano, in his *Memorie Sacre* (A.D. 1630), says that the tablet was much smaller at that time than when it was found: not only had time and the action of the atmosphere for 137 years consumed it, but portions had been cut off and sent to Toulouse and other churches.

"It is now," says Severano, "enclosed in a tabernacle with a glass before it, and only a few letters can be seen of the Hebrew; one Latin word only, NAZARENVS, and a letter or two of the following word; the remainder, as well in Greek as in Latin, is all gone."

When Suarez (1548-1617) visited Rome after the Council of Trent, he said that the word *Judaeorum* had gone, but he saw in Hebrew, Greek, and Latin the words IESVS NAZARENVS REX. He ascribes the loss of the *Judaeorum* to the divine will.

The present appearance of the relic is of a decayed piece of board ten inches long on which traces of the three languages remain. The Hebrew is quite illegible; only the lower parts of a few letters remain visible on the upper edge of the tablet. The Greek, or rough transliteration of Greek letters—NAZARENOVS B— and the Latin—AZARENVS RE—are still readable, although in the Latin decay has consumed the N in *Nazarenus* and the X in *Rex*; and in the Greek the greater part of *Basileus* is gone. The Greek word ΝαζαρενουS is misspelt, having ε for η, and ουS for oS. That which we read as B, the first letter of βαδιλευS, has also been deciphered as *I*; if the latter is correct, it in no way alters the sense of the inscription, which would then read Ιονδαύων βαδιλευS.

The Greek and Latin lines read from the right to the left after the custom of Hebrew writings. From this it is conjectured

Fig. 7: The Superscription (Santa Croce, Rome).

that a Jew, an illiterate mechanic, engraved the inscription for Pilate.

The letters are cut into the wood, not written on it. Alban Butler (1710-1773) says that, when found, the board was painted white, and the letters red, but that the colors have faded. At the present day there is no trace of color or varnish; it has only the appearance of old perishing wood; but what kind of wood it is cannot now be determined.

On Easter Sunday it is always exhibited with great pomp.

In the Church of Our Lady in Toulouse is an inscription that Butler says is an imitation of that preserved at Rome, but this inscription is in five lines, whereas the original has but three. We have seen how a piece was severed from the Inscription that is in Santa Croce and sent to Toulouse, which, being inserted into the new wood containing the whole inscription would—according to the customary use of relics—give it the reputation of the true Inscription.

8

THE NAILS

The accounts of the finding of the Nails used in the Crucifixion of Christ all agree in stating that they were discovered by St. Helena. Beyond this primary point, however, they considerably differ. Some say they were found at the same time as the Cross; others that they were not found until afterward. St. Gregory of Tours says the latter; the historian Socrates asserts that they were found at the same time.

In addition to this variance, we encounter the contradictory statements as to the number of nails used. The profane authors, when speaking on this subject, always mention four nails, which view is supported by many early ecclesiastical historians. St. Gregory of Tours, in his work already referred to on the glories of the martyrs, says that two nails were fixed in the hands and two in the feet. St. Cyprian (c. 200-258), St. Augustine (354-430), Pope Innocent III (c. 1160-1216), and Theodoret (c. 393-458) agree with him. On the other hand, St. Gregory Nazianzen (c. 329-390) intimates that only three were used, and Nonnus, a Greek poet of the fifth century, describes one foot as being placed over the other and both fastened with one nail.

RELICS FROM THE CRUCIFIXION

So far as art may be taken as evidence for the number of nails, early examples support the opinions of the majority of early writers. It is interesting to see how primitive crucifixes are portrayed, although they must not be accepted as authoritative.

The earliest known crucifixes in the catacombs, in the cemeteries of St. Julius or St. Valentine, in the Via Flaminia, attributed to the seventh or eighth century, have the feet separate, thus necessitating four nails.

A crucifix of the eighth century preserved at Lucca, carved in cedar wood—one of the three attributed to the handiwork of Nicodemus—shows our Lord crowned with a royal diadem and habited in a long robe reaching to the ankles. The feet, which are shod, are separate.

Another crucifix in cedar, attributed to St. Luke, which is at Siroli, near Ancona, also has the feet apart.

A crucifix in mosaic, consecrated by Pope John VII (650-707) in the old basilica of St. Peter in 706, represented the feet separate and fixed with two nails. Another of silver, in the treasury of the same church, which was given by Charlemagne to Pope Leo III (750-816) in the year 800, at the time of his coronation in Rome, has four nails. Pope Julius III (1487-1555) melted this crucifix to raise money, but caused a mold to be taken before doing so.

On an ivory triptych (c. 888) from the monastery of Rambona, now in the Vatican Museum, the carving of the Crucifixion represents four nails.

In those at Monza and Pisa, both very ancient, four nails are used. So it is in crucifixes of the Greek Church, whose unvarying conservatism often guides one to a correct solution of similar questions.

In the thirteenth century, three nails only are shown. Cimabue (c. 1240-1302) and Margaritone (c. 1250-1290) at

Fig. 8: Crucifixion of Jesus by Gustave Doré.

Florence first represented the Savior's feet laid one on the other. Jacques de Voragine (c. 1230-1298) first mentions the change; and Ayala, bishop of Galicia, credits the Albigensian heretics with being the first to declare that only three nails were used.

St. Helena sent to her imperial son at Constantinople the Nails that she had found. He had one of them attached to his helmet and another made into a bit for his horse, which, according to several of the Fathers—St. Cyril of Alexandria (c. 376-444), St. Ambrose, Theodoret, and others—was in fulfillment of the prophecy of Zechariah, "In that day that which is upon the bridle of the horse shall be holy to the Lord" (14:20, Douay-Rheims). St. Jerome, however, says in reference to this application of Holy Writ, "You often speak feelingly, indeed with piety, yet ridiculously."[8]

> *In bridle of King Constantine*
> *was no crystal as bright*
> *nor so brilliant to man's sight;*
> *Whitherso he feared that sire*
> *the bridle brightness bare of fire;*
> *many that saw that bridle bright*
> *turned to the grace of God's might.*[9]

St. Gregory of Tours accounts for the four Nails in this wise: one was made into a bit by the empress for her son's horse; another was placed in his helmet; the third St. Helena threw into the Adriatic Sea during a tempest, after which there was an immediate calm; and the fourth was fixed in the head of the statue of Constantine.

The Nails were preserved in Constantinople until the year 550, and the holy bit until the thirteenth century. There is no doubt that some — or parts — were carried into the West by St. Gregory the Great when he was legate of the Holy See to the Eastern Empire.

A Nail was deposited in a church built at Constantine's expense at Nakalakew, in Georgia. The kingdom of Georgia was highly favored by Constantine, who took pleasure in translating some of the most valued relics to a people brought within the fold of the Church, especially by the mission of St. Nina of Cappadocia (c. 296-c. 340). He sent to the newly converted King Mirian (c. 277-361), of the race of Chosroes, the footrest of the

---

[8] *Commentary on Zechariah.*
[9] *How the Holy Cross Was Found by St. Helen.*

Cross, and one of the Nails. These were brought from Georgia to Moscow by King Artchil in 1686 and are now preserved in the Synod of the Ascension in that city. The Nail is set in a royal crown of thirteenth-century workmanship, made by order of David, king of all Georgia, as is recorded in the Greek inscription engraved on it.

The Nail that had been fashioned into a bit for Constantine's horse was, after his death, placed in the imperial treasury with the other relics. In the year 553, during the fifth General Council and the second of Constantinople, convoked by the emperor Justinian (c. 482-565), Pope Vigilius (d. 555) took an oath upon these Nails: "His holiness Pope Vigilius has sworn to the very pious emperor in our presence (that is to say, the presence of us, Theodore of Caesarea in Cappadocia and Cethegus, patrician) by the virtue of the *holy nails* with which our Lord has been crucified, and by the four Evangelists."

We know that some of the Nails were retained at Constantinople in this same century in the cure effected by them on Justinian in 576. This contradicts the report attributing to St. Siffrein the honor of enriching his church with so precious a

Fig. 9: The Holy Bit of Carpentras.

relic, as he was at this time dead; it was most probably removed at the time of the Crusades.

The first authentic knowledge we have of this wonderful bit being at Carpentras in Provence, France, is in 1204. There is a deed in the archives of the diocese dated 1226, to which a *bulla* is attached bearing the figure of a nail, which is also on an instrument of the Hotel de Ville of 1250, showing how greatly the privilege of its possession was appreciated. Mention is made of it in an inventory of relics in 1322; and it was refashioned during the sojourn of the popes at Avignon, 1309 to 1379.

The Iron Crown of Lombardy is so called from an iron ring or band within the circlet of gold, a crown that is held in great veneration. In the first place, it is revered on account of its great antiquity and associations: Gregory the Great is said to have given it to Theodelinda (c. 570-628), a Frankish princess, under whom the Lombards were convinced of the errors of Arianism and embraced the Catholic Faith, and she bequeathed it to the church of Monza at her death in 628.

Secondly, because the iron band is said to be beaten out of one of the Nails of the True Cross that Helena gave to Constantine — an assertion that scarcely bears historical test. This crown, of acknowledged antiquity, was known as the Corona Aurea, the golden crown, until the time of Otho IV (c. 1174-1218). The tradition that this iron band was one of the Holy Nails cannot be traced beyond the latter part of the sixteenth century. Pope Julius II in 1464 mentions the existence of this iron, but with no reference to its sanctity; in fact, rather contemptuously than otherwise.[10] Burgatus is the first to mention its sacred associations (1587); but two years before his publication, the archpriest

[10] *Hist. Aust.*, 1:iv.

of Monza speaks of it as a most precious possession of the Church, not on account of the iron, but as being used at the coronations of Charlemagne, Henry of Luxemburg, and the early Teutonic Roman emperors. The sanctity of the crown was discredited by the historian Muratori (1672-1750). The ecclesiastical authorities could not agree upon it: decrees and counterdecrees directed it to be sometimes adored as a sacred relic and sometimes regarded as a state trophy until in 1688 the question was referred to the Congregation of Rites. The inquiry was protracted until 1717, which, after all, left the crucial point untouched, although it pronounced in favor of its being exposed for adoration and carried in processions.

Bellani, canon of Monza, asserts that the golden crown and the iron band were formerly distinct, that the Holy Nail was that fixed to the helmet of Constantine and at some later time placed in the Byzantine crown. Muratori considers it to have been a piece of ordinary iron, inserted into the crown to give stability to the golden plates of which it is composed.

Among the presents sent by Hugh the Great to our Saxon King Athelstan by Adulph of Flanders was the reputed sword of Constantine, in the pommel of which, set in massive gold, was an iron spike, "one of the four which were prepared for the Crucifixion of our Lord."

The following localities boast the possession of fragments of the Nails of the Crucifixion: Aix-la-Chapelle; Ancône (Cathedral); Arras; Bamberg; Bavaria; Carpentras; Catane, Sicily; Colle, Tuscany; Cologne; Compiègne; Cracovie, Poland; the Escorial; Florence; Lagny; Milan; Monza; Naples; Nuremberg; Paris; Rome (Santa Croce); Rome (St. Marie in Campitelli); Siena; Spoleto; Torcello; Torno; Toul; Trier; Troyes; Venice; and Vienna. This remarkable multiplication of the Nails, distributed throughout

Europe, demands some explanation. Much that is said in such explanation, however, seems to be but an excuse for the desire of so many places to possess relics closely associated with our Lord's Passion. There is no doubt that with these, as with the thorns, spurious "true nails" have been manufactured to satisfy such cravings.

In the first place, there may have been many nails employed in the construction of the Cross, the fastening of the transverse beam, the rest for the feet, and the inscription, in addition to those that pierced our Lord's body, all of which would legitimately be termed nails from the Cross. Another explanation, however, and more truly adhering to the Holy Nails that actually pierced the Redeemer, is found in the statement that, for the wider distribution of the *four* Nails found by St. Helena, Constantine caused them to be wrought into twelve smaller

nails, an account largely received in early days. A further explanation is that many new nails were made, and in them a few filings from the true Nails were inserted, which thus constituted true relics. The Nail in Santa Croce, Rome, which was pronounced by Pope Benedict XIV (1758-1769) to be authentic, shows manifest signs of having been filed.

Fig. 10: Holy Nails—left: Santa Maria in Campitelli, Rome; right: Trier. The point is at Toul.

Fig. 11: Holy Nail (Santa Croce, Rome).

The multiplication of Nails by St. Charles Borromeo (1538-1584) appears unwarranted and seems averse to his known holiness of life. It is said that he had many nails made like the true one preserved at Milan. After they had been touched or blessed with the Holy Nail, they were distributed as original. He sent one as a relic to Philip II (1527-1598), king of Spain.

At the time of the Revolution in France, M. Lelièvre obtained permission to take the Nail preserved in Paris to analyze and examine it as an object of mineralogy. He returned it in 1827 to the archbishop of Paris with an assurance on oath that it was the veritable Nail he had received from the treasury of St. Denis. In this way, and by this excuse, he had reverently guarded it from the profanation it would otherwise have received from the blasphemous mob.

The Saxon poem in the aforementioned *Vercelli Codes*, after describing the finding of the Cross, makes Helena bid the converted Jew to search for the Nails. He went to Calvary and prayed for a token revealing the spot:

> *There came suddenly*
> *brighter than the sun*
> *a dancing fire.*
> *The people saw*

RELICS FROM THE CRUCIFIXION

their Lord of grace
perform a miracle:

when there, out of the darkness
like stars of heaven
or jewels,
close to the ground,
the nails from out of their prison
shining below
flashed with light.

He took the nails,
sickening with fear,
and to the venerable
queen he brought them.

St. Helena then sent for a very wise man to advise her to what use she might most worthily employ the nails. He answered:

"Command thou the nails —
for the noblest
of earthly kings,
of palace-owners —
on his bridle to set,
the bit of his steed;
that shall to many
throughout the world
become famous,
when in the fight;
with them
he shall overcome
every one of his foes.

The Nails

It shall be known
that the king's horse shall (go)
under the proud one,
adorned with bits,
with bridle rings.

That good beacon shall be
called holy,
and the brave-minded one
honored in war
whom that horse beareth."

Then that speedily
all performed
Elene, before the men;
she commanded the noble one's,
the ring-giver of men's,
bridle to deck,
her own son's.

She sent it as a present
over the ocean stream,
a blameless gift.

THE CROWN OF THORNS

Except in the Bible, the Crown of Thorns is not mentioned by any writer during the first four hundred years. It is supposed to have been hidden, but St. Paulinus, bishop of Nola (409-431), speaks of its existence as a well-known fact. St. Gregory of Tours is, however, the first to speak explicitly of it.

About the year 800 the patriarch of Jerusalem sent to Charlemagne a Nail, a piece of the Cross, and some of the Thorns from the Crown. These relics were given to the Abbey of St. Denis by Charles the Bald (823-877); an inscription on his tomb recorded this donation.

At the time of the First Crusade, Alexius Commenus (c. 1050-1118) wrote to Count Robert of Flanders, describing the many precious relics that were in the city of Constantinople, thinking thereby to persuade the Latins to consider the defense of that place incumbent on them as containing memorials of our Lord's Passion, for the preservation of which all Christians should count their lives as naught. This was cunningly urged at the time when Western Christendom was burning to rescue holy places from the desecration of the infidel. Among these relics, he mentioned the column to which Christ was bound for flagellation, the lash with which He was scourged, the purple robe, the Crown of Thorns, the reed, mockingly placed in His hand for a scepter, a piece of the Cross, some of the Nails, and the linen cloths found in the Sepulcher on that first Easter morn.

After the advent of the Latin rulers over the Byzantine Empire, the condition of that state was not enviable. Baldwin II (1217-1273), expelled by his subjects from the throne of Constantinople, wandered through the European courts to solicit aid for the recovery of his dominions. The pope, Gregory IX (1145-1241), was naturally disposed to espouse his cause; and the Byzantine Crusade was preached in the Papal States with greater earnestness than that which at the same time was arming for the rescue of Palestine.

Louis IX of France (1214-1270) granted to the mendicant emperor large confiscations from the Jews. Baldwin had also borrowed from the Venetians a sum of money on the security of the Crown of Thorns. But his necessities demanded a yet larger supply, which, in order to gain, he had to abandon altogether the treasure that had hitherto been only pawned. He addressed a letter to Louis of France, asking his "dear cousin and benefactor" to pay the loan thus contracted and to supply him with further funds in exchange for the holy relic.

Louis, by the advice of his ministers, undertook to redeem from Nicolo Quirini and other Venetian and Genoese merchants, to whom it had been pledged, that most precious relic of the Eastern capital: the Crown of Thorns.

On the payment of 13,134 perperi (about £6,567 in 1910) to the Italians and 10,000 livres to Baldwin himself, the bargain was closed. There were, however, certain difficulties to be overcome. The Abbey of St. Denis already boasted one Crown of Thorns, the genuineness of which had been proved by miracles. Some people thought this obstacle by no means insuperable, while others of the present day consider that it condemns the verity of both relics; but, as we have seen, a morsel of a true relic inserted into a model of the whole always assumed the full title, and doubtless the Crown already possessed by the Abbey of St. Denis consisted of those thorns given to the abbey by Charles the Bald. Another obstacle was the conscientious scruples of Louis against the commission of simony, a sin that included the bartering of relics, yet which received the countenance of many of the highest ecclesiastics. Baldwin, however, evaded this by making over the Crown of Thorns to the French king "freely and gratuitously" and by receiving equally gratuitously a free gift of money sufficient to meet his wants.

After the adjustment of these preliminaries, two Dominican monks, James and Andrew, were sent to Venice. One of these brethren had been in a monastery in Constantinople, where he had frequently seen this Crown of Thorns and was well informed in all concerning the emperor Baldwin. They were accompanied by an official with letters charging the keepers to deliver the relic to these, the king's ambassadors. Before redeeming the relic, they took all precautions to confirm its authenticity. The seals were carefully examined and found intact, and they affixed their own seals in addition.

Vincent of Beauvais (c. 1190-c. 1264) and other historians relate in detail the events of the journey. After a successful voyage, which at this time of the year, Gosselin remarks, was a serious undertaking, having embarked near Christmastide, they arrived in France, and traveled to Villeneuve l'Archevêque, five leagues from Sens. Here they were met on August 10, 1239, by St. Louis IX, accompanied by his queen-mother, his brothers, many prelates, and nobles of the court, who had proceeded

*Fig. 12: The Crown of Thorns brought
into France (fifteenth century).*

thus far from Paris to do honor to the sacred Crown. The king
and his second brother, Robert of Artois (1216-1250), barefoot
and in their shirts, carried it into the Cathedral of St. Stephen,
in Sens.

The wooden case was here opened, and the seals and docu-
ments attesting its authenticity examined. The following day
the king and his court returned to Paris, where, eight hours later,
the solemn reception took place. The king and his brother again

bore it amid a brilliant escort and enthusiastic populace, chanting hymns and litanies, first to Notre Dame, and afterward to the Chapel of St. Nicholas within the precincts of the palace.

Sometime after this translation, St. Louis received from Baldwin a piece of the Cross and other relics. To provide a fitting shrine for these memorials of the Passion, the king built the Sainte Chapelle on the site of the ancient chapel of the Palais de Justice. It was begun in 1241 and finished in 1248, at a cost of about £800,000. Few edifices in Europe have excited more interest, or been visited with a more profound reverence, than this most beautiful structure, which yet remains an example to this matter-of-fact age. The disregard of expense when the honor of our Lord—through reeds and wood believed to have borne Him, or to have been borne by Him—called for the devotion of his children is here exemplified. The spire of this architectural gem was burned in 1620 but was replaced by another in 1853, quite in harmony with the rest of the building.

At almost the same time, in 1230, by a singular coincidence, a similar chapel was built by the Pisans—Santa Maria del Ponte—which was destined to enshrine a similar relic. A merchant of Pisa brought from the Holy Land a thorn from the Crown, which was presented to this church by his descendants in 1333, when the dedication of the chapel was changed to Santa Maria della Spina. It is, like the Sainte Chapelle of Paris, a marvel of architecture. In the chapels of Paris and of Pisa the reliquaries have been destroyed through the lust for gold, but the relics have been preserved.

The relics in the Sainte Chapelle were kept there until the Revolution. From the foundation until 1656, the keys of the shrine were kept by the king himself or by one of the nobles delegated by him.

RELICS FROM THE CRUCIFIXION

When Paris was in the hands of the mob, the Crown of Thorns was carried to the Abbey of St. Denis for safety by order of Louis XVI in 1791 but was brought back to Paris in 1793 and deposited in the Hotel des Monnaies; the following year it was placed in the Bibliothèque Nationale and finally taken to the cathedral of Notre Dame by order of the government, on October 26, 1804.

The Crown is a circlet of shrunken reeds bound together, but without a single thorn remaining. The diameter of the interior of the ring is 210 millimeters, and the section is 15 millimeters; the section of each reed is 1 to 1.5 millimeters in diameter.

It is mounted in a ring of crystal: the crystal is in six pieces, which are kept in position by three leaves of bronze, gilt.

To understand how this bundle of thornless reeds formed the Crown of Thorns, it is necessary to disassociate the mind from representations of our Lord's Passion, which the brush or the chisel place constantly before us, and conceive, not a circle of thorns but a veritable crown, or bonnet, which would cover the crown of the head of the divine Victim. This bundle of reeds, evidently grown in water or marshy ground, is supposed to have formed the fillet to give shape to the diadem of thorns, and to have passed around the forehead, plaited around and above with the pliable

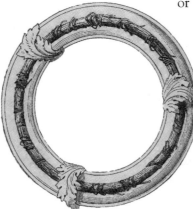

Fig. 13: The Crown of Thorns (Paris).

branches of the Arabian nabk plant, which has strong and
sharp thorns, or the Rhamnus, called "Christ's Thorn," thus
forming a semicircular bonnet, called by Diez the *helmet* of the
Son of God. Some say that it was taken off at the same time
as the vestures, while others, among whom is Origen, support
the general idea that it remained on Christ's head while He
hung on the Cross.

Miss Margaret Stokes (1832-1900) held a theory that the
thorny diadem was placed on the sacred head to create not
pain but humiliation—a parody of the radiated crown worn by
the Roman emperors when they arrogated to themselves divin-
ity—that it was intended for an instrument of *moral* rather than
of *physical* suffering, and thus formed part of the mock regalia.

The poem "In Festo Coronae Domini" was written by Cardinal Bonaventura (1221-1274) in honor of the Crown of Thorns
and its acquisition by France and was used as a sequence in the
Mass of that feast in the Gallican and Sarum Missals.

> *Wouldst thou boast thyself aright*
> *And by God with glory bright*
> *In eminence be crowned?*

> *Learn this crown to venerate*
> *And His course to imitate*
> *Whose Brow it did surround.*

> *The King of heaven wore this crown*
> *And gave it honor and renown*
> *By His own sanctity:*

> *In this casque he fought the fight*
> *And put the ancient foe to flight*
> *And triumphed on the Tree.*

RELICS FROM THE CRUCIFIXION

A knightly helm in this we see
In this a palm of victory
    The High Priest's miter too:

Though with thorns 'twas first arrayed
Hallowed by that sacred head
    It bare a golden hue.

For the sharpness of the thorns
By His passion Christ adorns
    With rays of golden light:

Souls beset with thorns of sin,
Hopeless ever life to win,
    Find blessings infinite.

For the sinner thorns arise;
Of his own iniquities
    A thorny crown is twined:

But the thorns are changed to gold
When he turns and seeks the fold,
    That he may mercy find.

These are right mysterious joys;
But the matter that employs
    Our gratulations now.

Is the tale which doth convey
Signal fame to France today
    To decorate her brow.

To her care the Holy Crown
Is entrusted as her own,
    Whereof we keep the day.

The Crown of Thorns

All the honor that is due
With devotion yearly new
    Unto this feast we pay.

Holding such a priceless treasure
To be longed for above measure,
    Thou art enriched indeed;

Happy land beyond compare,
To the Lord exceeding dear,
    Unequaled is thy meed.

Other realms to thee concede
Three distinctions that exceed
    The honors they can claim.

Faith unfeigned, valor great,
Oil thy kings to consecrate;
    So flourisheth thy fame.

City of illustrious name,
Brilliant in thy peerless fame,
    Mother of studies dear;

Paris, the pride of Gallic race,
In thee the Crown hath found a place
    Which faithful men revere.

God's Holy Name to magnify
Thy utmost energies apply,
    This for thy duty own;

Palladium of Christ divine.
Selected for the sacred shrine
    Of that most holy Crown.

Relics from the Crucifixion

O Jesu gentle, Jesu mild,
To us when press'd in conflict wild
  Grant victory over sin:

So deign our lives to rule and guide,
That we who in thy aid confide,
  An endless crown may win.

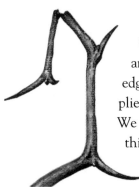

*Fig. 14: Holy Thorn
(Wevelghem).*

Among the number of thorns that exist, all being declared as from the True Crown, it is difficult to know which are the originals, as it is openly acknowledged that they have been greatly multiplied to satisfy the devotion of the faithful. We constantly find them sent hither and thither as valued gifts. Among those presents mentioned as being sent by Hugh to Athelstan was a small piece of the Crown of Thorns that the English king gave to the monastery of Malmesbury. St. Helena sent a branch of thorns to the city of Trier and two long thorns to her Church of Santa Croce at Rome. The Abbey of St. Denis received two contributions of thorns: from Charles the Bald in the ninth century and from Philip Augustus (1165-1223) in 1205. In this way thorns were distributed throughout Europe.

The following list of churches at the present time possessing thorns, branches of thorns, or fragments of the reeds, is taken from *Mémoire sur les instruments de la Passion* by M. de Fleury, who carefully searched the treasuries far and near for these mementoes of the Passion. From the appearance of the fillet and the small number of churches possessing pieces of the reeds, we may rest assured that very few have been taken from the jealously guarded Crown at Notre Dame.

Relics of the reeds (or rushes) remain at: Arras, Autun, Chablis, Lyon, Paris, and Vaugirard.

Branches remain at: Andechs, Bavaria (4), Munich (5), Pisa (3), Trier (5), Venice (2), Le Villars (3), and Wevelghem, Belgium (3).

Simple thorns are preserved at: Andrea (1), Angers (1), Autun (3), Baume (1), Besançon (2), Bordeaux (1), Bourbon-l'Archambault (1), Bruges (1), Brussels (1), Carpentras (1), Chalette (1), Châlons (1), Chelles (1), Cluny (1), Colle (2), Compiègne (1), Cuisery (3), Fermo (1), Florence (6), Fontainebleau (1), Ghent (1), Gray (1), Lagny (1), Libourne (1), Longpont (1), Melun (1), Milan (4), Nice (2), Paris (8), Perpignan (7), Pontarlier (1), Raguse (1), Rheims (1), Rome (19), St. Acheul (1), St. Étienne en Forez (1), Solesmes (1), Stanbrook (3), Soleilmont, Belgium (1), Tarraga (2), Toledo (1), and Toulouse (1).

We have seen how the preservation and distribution of these relics gave birth to arts that otherwise might never have been conceived. The reliquary that encloses that part of the Crown of Thorns possessed by Arras, preserved in the Convent of the

Fig. 15: Reliquary of the Holy Thorn (Arras).

RELICS FROM THE CRUCIFIXION

Augustine Sisters, is of the most exquisite thirteenth-century brasswork, a representation of which conveys a better idea of its beauty than is possible by any description. In delicacy of workmanship it is unsurpassed, though in elaborate detail it must give place to the reliquary of the Holy Blood at Bruges.

Among the costly relics in a convent at Valladolid was a brick or slab of massive gold, nearly a foot in length and an inch thick, which contained one of the holy thorns. During Napoleon Bonaparte's campaign, one of his generals seized this costly object and presented it to the emperor, who, taking out the thorn, said: "There, give that back to the monks; I keep the brick."

10

THE HOLY LANCE

In the apocryphal *Gospel of Nicodemus* it was said that it was a soldier named Longinus who pierced our Savior's side with a spear as He hung on the Cross. André de Crete (c. 650-c. 740) gives a traditional report that the Lance, or Spear, was found at the same time and in the same place as the Cross, the Nails, and other instruments of the Passion.

St. Gregory of Tours says that after the Crucifixion, the Spear was kept in Jerusalem until the city was taken by the Persians, when the emperor Heraclius had it brought to Constantinople, in the early part of the seventh century.

In the time of the Venerable Bede, a spearhead, professedly that used by Longinus, was enclosed in a cross of wood and pre-served beneath the porch of the Church of the Martyrs, built by Constantine.

The spear of Charlemagne that Hugh sent to King Athelstan, was said to be — or to contain part of — that which pierced our Lord's side. This spear, it was averred, through its divine associa-tion, always assured victory to Charles when he used it in battle and retained its efficacy in the just combat of Guy of Warwick with Colbrand the Dane.

Fig. 16: Lance Piercing the Side of Jesus by Fra Angelico.

Thus we see it was venerated long before it was again said to have been discovered in the eleventh century in this wise: during the first Crusade, when the Christian garrison in Antioch was closely besieged and famine was reducing the inhabitants, despair was usurping courage when an event is said to have happened that again revived the drooping spirits, inspired enthusiasm, and led to victory. On the morning of Wednesday, June 9, 1098, Count Raymond and Adhemar, bishop of Puy, were sadly gazing from the ramparts on the surrounding hosts of Corbogha, when Peter Bartholomew of Provence (d. 1099) craved an interview. He told a strange story of how the apostle St. Andrew had appeared to him in a dream and bade him tell the princes how he had revealed to him the hiding place of the very lance that had pierced the Savior's side. Placing no credence in the dream, he neglected its monition. Then the vision was repeated. Fear, he said, deterred his approach to the nobles. He fled from the city and sailed for Cyprus, but, being driven back by a storm, he dared no longer keep silent, and declared the spearhead to be hidden beneath the Church of the Prince of the Apostles.

The count, unlike the bishop, professed to believe the story and gave Peter into the care of his chaplain. That same night, the vision was confirmed to the priest Stephen, who was watching—or sleeping—in the Church of St. Mary, when Christ Himself promised aid in five days.

On the fifth day, early in the morning, Raymond of Agiles, the aforementioned chaplain and recorder of this event, with eleven others, went to the Church of St. Peter. The whole day they were digging in relays but with no result. "At last, seeing that we were fatigued, the young man who had told us of the lance leapt into the pit, all ungirt as he was, without shoes and in his shirt. He adjured us to call upon God to render us the lance. And I, who have written these things, as soon as ever the blade appeared above ground, greeted it with a kiss; nor can I tell how great joy and exultation then filled the city."

This so-called discovery was made by twelve irresponsible people, for we hear of the presence of neither a prelate nor a noble. Many of the well informed would know the existence of an accepted spearhead, and the reputation of Charlemagne's lance, although probably the desire for something to dissipate the apathy of their troops determined the generals to leave things to take their course without their interference. The fraud was perpetrated, and it had the desired effect: it revived the spirits of

Fig. 17: Discovery of the Holy Lance (nineteenth century).

the depressed. They fought with renewed vigor and conquered. If we are doubtful of the veracity of the said Peter, it is but in company with many of his comrades and contemporaries who, as will be seen, put him through an ordeal for his truth's sake.

The Crusaders issued from the city on the morning of the twenty-eighth to attack the enemy, and Raymond continues, "As we marched from the bridge toward the mountains it was a toilsome journey, for the enemy strove to hem us in. Yet though we of the bishop's squadron were hard pressed in the fight, thanks to the Lord's lance, none of us were wounded, no, not so much as by an arrow. I, who speak these things, saw them for myself, since I was bearing the Lord's lance."

Corbogha was defeated, the victory was complete.

It has been related how bishop Adhemar was skeptical when he heard Peter's story, so Peter related another dream to support his former statements. The bishop died on August 1, and on the night after his burial in St. Peter's Church, he appeared to Peter Bartholomew in company with Christ and St. Andrew. He confessed that he had been taken down into hell in punishment for his doubts as to the Holy Lance, but that after his entombment Christ had visited him in the flames and brought him up to heaven, whence he now appeared.

The matter did not end here. Other visions followed. Peter evidently yearned after a reputation. He gained it, but not for sanctity. His stories were ridiculed by many. Prominent among the scoffers was Arnulf, chaplain to Robert of Normandy, who afterward became patriarch of Jerusalem. Peter defended himself by demanding the ordeal by fire: "Make me the biggest fire you can," said he, "and I will pass through its midst with the Lord's Lance in my hand. If it be the Lord's Lance may I pass through unharmed; if not, may I be burned up."

According to Raymond the chaplain, on the morning of Good Friday, April 8, 1099, forty thousand spectators assembled to see the ordeal. The fire was fed by two parallel piles of dead olive branches fourteen feet long and four feet in height, with a path one foot wide between them.

When the fires were kindled, I, Raymond, spake before the multitude: "If God hath spoken to this man Peter face-to-face and if the blessed Andrew showed him the Lord's Lance as he slept, may he pass through the fire unharmed; but if the thing be a lie, let him be burned up altogether with the Lance that he holds." And all the people answered, "Amen." Now the fire blazed so fiercely that it occupied the space of twenty cubits, nor could any man approach it.

Then Peter, kneeling before the bishop of Albara, received the Lance and manfully entered the fire. As he issued from the flames the multitude hailed him with loud cries of "God aid him" and became so enthusiastic that had not Raymond forced his way through the throng to save him Peter would, in the excitement, have been pulled to pieces.

In a few days Peter died, and the ordeal but confirmed both the credulous and the incredulous in their respective beliefs. The credulous asserted that he had not been burned up altogether with the Lance that he held, while the incredulous affirmed that he had not survived the trial, but his death was caused by the fire. Even Raymond, who had championed him throughout, acknowledged that "there was some sign of burning about him."

In the Arthurian legends of the Holy Grail, a lance figures in the procession before the dumb-stricken Sir Galahad in the castle of the Fisher king. This feature was first introduced into the legend by Chrestien, without mentioning its origin; but his continuators identified it, without hesitation, with the Spear of the Crucifixion. This may have been Chrestien's idea, suggested perhaps by the reported discovery of the Lance at Antioch half a century before.

In 1243 the emperor Baldwin II sent the point of the Spear to Venice as a pledge for a loan. St. Louis of France redeemed this relic along with others by paying the sum and interest and had it brought to Paris. It was preserved in the Sainte Chapelle until the year 1793, when it was taken to the Bibliothèque Nationale. In 1796 the Abbé Coterel examined it and in his report states that it was more than three inches in length and was pointed at one extremity. This piece is now lost.

The remainder of the True Lance was in 1492 sent by Bajazet, the Turkish sultan, to Pope Innocent VIII (1432-1492), by the hand of Pierre d'Aubusson (1423-1503), Grand Master of the Knights of Rhodes. It was in a rich case, and the sultan added that the point was in the possession of the king of France. Here for once are two authorities agreeing in their statements. Innocent placed it in the treasury of the old St. Peter's in Rome with the *volto santo*, where it was held in great veneration. It is now in one of the great piers of the present Church of St. Peter, and in front of it, over an image of Longinus is inscribed, "THE SPEAR OF LONGINUS, which Innocent VIII, Chief Pontiff, received from Bajazet, the Sultan of the Turks; Urban VIII (c. 1568-1644) transferred it to a decorated shrine, raising an image and erecting a shrine beneath."

In the rock-hewn monastery of Kickaert, or Kickart, not far from Erivan, Armenia, another professedly true lance is preserved, said to have been brought into Armenia by St. Matthew. It is held in the greatest veneration and is shown to pilgrims, by request, at the close

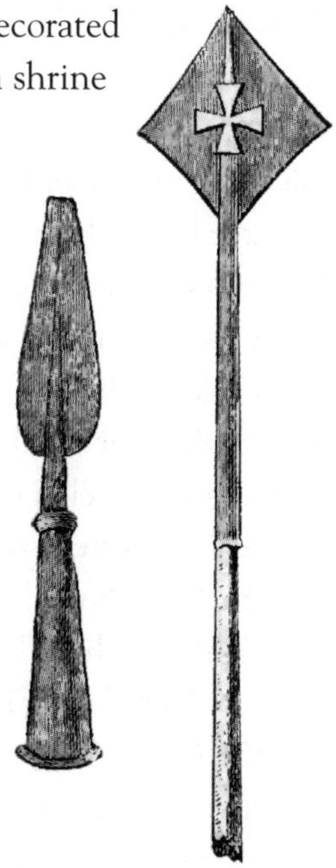

Fig. 18: The Holy Lance—left: St. Peter's, Rome; right: Kickaert, Erivan. Ancona also claims to possess part of the original Lance.

of Mass. Crude in form, the lozenge-shaped head, 2 3/8 inches wide, is pierced with a cross; it fails to resemble in shape the spearhead of any age or nation. It is possible that it might have been wrought out of a fragment, or that some filings of the True Lance were welded into it, but this theory they will not admit. It does, however, resemble the "Holy Lance" used by the priest in the ritual of the Mass in the Eastern Church.

An altogether erroneous idea is perpetuated in the constantly repeated saying that the Lance of the Passion is at Nuremberg, under the name of the Holy Lance. The known history of that relic contradicts the false tradition. It is actually known as the Holy Lance of St. Maurice and is preserved in the Imperial Museum in Vienna. It is a long spearhead of iron, socketed to fit on a staff. A hole was pierced in the blade, probably about the time of Otho (d. 973), and a Nail is said to be one taken from the Cross, inserted therein. It was, perhaps, during this operation that the spearhead was broken and a ligature of thin iron plates applied; this being insufficient, it was strengthened by a band of iron. The emperor Henry III had a band of silver placed over that of iron, which is inscribed: "Clavus Domini + Henricus Di gra Tercius Romanorum Imperator Aug. Hoc Argentum Jussit"; and on the other side: "Fabricari ad confirmacionem Clavi Dni et Lanceae Sancti Mauricii"; and in the middle: "Sanctus Mauricius."

During the reign of Charles IV (1347-1378), the silver was covered by a plate of gold, inscribed, "Lancea et Clavus Domini"; and the blade bound by silver wire to keep the fractured Spear and Nail together. The golden plate becoming loose, the inscribed silver plate of Henry III was revealed, and also the loss of half the Nail; and it is conjectured that the relic-collecting propensities of Charles IV caused that monarch to add the golden covering to hide his acquisition of half the Nail.

Our first knowledge of this relic is from the pen of Widu-kind (c. 923-973), a monk of the Abbey of Carbie, who tells us that it was in the possession of Constantine the Great and that it formed part of the regalia of Conrad; that in the hand of Otho, his troops were led to victory in the battles of Bierten and Lechfeld; and that it was delivered to Henry II to substantiate his claim to the throne.

It was kept at Vienna until 1423, when it was sent for safety to Nuremberg; there it remained a long time, and, when it was returned to Vienna, an exact replica was made and kept in the city of its refuge.

Thus, it will be seen that the claim for it is as a relic of the Holy Nails and not of the Spear, and that it is at Vienna, while only a model is preserved at Nuremberg.

THE HOLY BLOOD

Some places have proudly claimed the possession of portions of that life-giving blood poured out for our salvation on the tree of Crucifixion. They profess to own drops of that original stream from the pierced side and affirm that it is not from the consecrated chalice that opens to all Catholics the privilege of receiving that veritable blood.

There is no historical trace of the preservation of this divine relic in early days. It is well known that the custom prevailed among early Christians of preserving the blood of their martyrs, which was but a continuation of the usage of the Hebrews when their friends suffered the penalty of the law. Therefore there is every probability that our Savior's blood was eagerly caught by his disciples. Early mention of its preservation belongs to mythical literature. There were two old legends respecting it: one that it was received into vessels by the Blessed Virgin and St. John as it flowed from the wounds; the other, that it was collected by Nicodemus and Joseph of Arimathea when they took down the body from the Cross and placed it in the tomb.

The Arthurian legends supply us with stories, at one time largely credited, of the original custodian of our Lord's blood.

RELICS FROM THE CRUCIFIXION

The Holy Grail and its quest supplied material for many a romance, and the number of manuscripts on the subject shows how popular it had become. These various accounts, so much alike, prove them to have sprung from one original source.

The Holy Grail was said to be the vessel used by our Lord at the Institution of the Eucharist and was given by Pilate to Joseph of Arimathea, who in it received the Blood of Christ as it flowed from his blessed wounds. In the intercalation in Gautier, we are told that Joseph caught the Blood from the two feet. The so-called *Grand Saint Graal* says the vessel received the Blood that gushed from the body when it was taken from the Cross. When Joseph was imprisoned, the Holy Grail miraculously sustained him, and, when exiled, he brought the treasure to Marseilles and thence to Britain. At his death he begged that the Grail might remain in his family, that none but his seed should possess it. It was confided to his brother-in-law Brons and passed to his second son Josue, in whose line it remained.

Then follows the quest by Arthur's knights. The hermit-uncle of Perceval tells him how his race is so loved by Christ that he committed His Blood to their keeping. It passes into Perceval's possession when he succeeds to his uncle's crown, but after his death, it was nevermore seen, from which circumstance it was supposed that the Grail, Lance, and Dish were carried up to heaven, man having fallen so far below the ideal that he was no longer worthy of the presence of the holiest of the holy.

These legends, be it noticed, ignore the other traditions. Some say the Holy Grail, by St. Joseph's desire, was buried with him in his grave; others relate it to Chalice Hill, just outside the ancient precincts of the Abbey at Glastonbury, where it is said the sacred cup was hidden and from which hill arises an endless flow of healing water, which marks its course with a red deposit. It is called the Blood Well to the present day.

Among the churches possessing portions of the precious Blood, the most famous were Rome's Santa Croce in Jerusalemme, St. Mary the Great (where it is kept in a crystal in a cross of wood), and in the table of relics at St. John Lateran, where there are two phials containing the treasure. All these are in Rome, but the same relic is at Bruges in Belgium and the Abbey of Fécamp in France. In England, Glastonbury, Westminster, Hailes (in Gloucestershire), and Ashbridge (in Buckinghamshire) were enriched with similar relics.

In 1247 King Henry III ordered all the nobles of England to assemble at Westminster on the feast of the Translation of the Relics of St. Edward "to hear the most agreeable news of a holy benefit lately conferred by Heaven on the English people." They mustered in great force, wondering at such a message and speculating on its substance, no one able to enlighten another on the subject. Political matters occupied the expectant council for a considerable time, but at last, these being disposed of, they inquired what was that agreeable news they had been summoned to hear. The king told them how he had caused them to assemble to make known how the country had acquired a most precious relic, which he had obtained from the patriarch of Jerusalem. This was nothing less than a portion of our Savior's Blood shed on Calvary, enclosed in a handsome crystalline vessel. The authenticity was unquestionable, as it had been entrusted to a well-known conscientious brother of the Temple by the Grand Master of the Templars and was sealed with the seals of the patriarch of Jerusalem, the archbishop, bishops, abbots, and other noblemen at that time in the Holy Land. This gift would be solemnly presented by the king at the altar of the Abbey Church of St. Peter on the following day. During that night the king kept watch, fasting, by the relic, around which tapers were kept burning.

King Henry had directed that all the priests of London should assemble, with due order and reverence, at St. Paul's Cathedral early in the morning of St. Edward's Day. They were to be vested, as for a festival, in their surplices and hoods (attended by their clerks also becomingly clad) and their symbols, crosses, and lighted tapers. Thither the king also went and received the treasure with the greatest reverence and honor. Clothed in a humble dress, consisting of a poor man's cloak without a hood, and preceded by the priests and clerks, he proceeded without stopping to the Abbey at Westminster. He walked the whole distance, holding the relic above his head that it might be publicly seen; his arms being supported by an attendant at either side, lest his strength should fail.

Matthew of Paris (1200-1259), the monk of St. Albans, was present and has given a detailed account of what he saw: "Nor should it be omitted to be mentioned that he carried it with both hands when he came to any rugged or uneven part of the road, and always kept his eyes fixed on heaven or on the vessel itself." The pall or canopy was borne over it on four spears.

Arriving at the gate of the bishop of Durham's court, the procession was met by the conventual chapter of Westminster, accompanied by all the bishops, abbots, and monks who had assembled in great numbers, singing, and—to use the chronicler's words—exulting in a holy spirit and with tears. They then proceeded to the church in the same order, but the multitude was so great that the church could scarcely hold them all. The king, however, did not stop, but unweariedly carrying the vessel as before, made the circuit of the church, the palace, and his own apartments. "Finally he presented and made an offer of it,

Fig. 19: Reception of the Holy Blood at Westminster.

as a priceless gift, and one that had made England illustrious to God, to the Church of St. Peter at Westminster, to his beloved Edward, and the holy brethren who at that place minister to God and the saints."

The bishop of Norwich sang the High Mass and also preached on that occasion. In his sermon he stated that "of all things held sacred among men, the most sacred is the Blood of Christ, for it was the price of the world, and the shedding of it was its salvation"; and in order to magnify the circumstances the more, he added that saying of the philosopher:

> Every end is higher than its means. In truth, the Cross is a most holy thing on account of the more holy shedding of Christ's blood made upon it, not the blood-shedding on account of the Cross. These things we believe that England might have as much joy and glory in the possession of this great treasure as France had felt in obtaining possession of the Holy Cross which the King of France reverenced, and not without good cause, loving it more than gold and jewels.

He also added:

It was on account of the great reverence and holiness
of the King of England, who was known to be the most
Christian of all Christian princes, that this invaluable
treasure, had been sent by the Patriarch of Jerusalem, in
order that it might be reverenced more in England than in
Syria, which was now left nearly desolate. For in England,
as the world knew, faith and holiness flourished more than
in any other country throughout the world.

A discussion arose among some of the congregation whether
the relic was genuine. Theodoric, prior of the Hospitallers of St.
John of Jerusalem, addressed himself to those present in these
words: "Why do you still hesitate, my dear lords? Does any one
of us, Templars, Hospitallers, or even the brother who brought
it, demand any benefit for the same? Does he ask any remunera-
tion in gold or silver from the king or anyone else, or even the
smallest reward?"

"By no means," replied the king.

"Why," again asked the monk, "should so many men of such
high rank, to the damnation of their own souls, bear testimony
to such an assertion and affix their seals to it, which are manifest
pledges of their good faith?"

These questions seemingly convinced the doubting multitude,
and the bishop of Norwich, after supporting the lay brother's
arguments, announced an indulgence of six years, one hundred
forty days to all who should devoutly come to worship the Holy
Blood.

The relics at Hailes and Ashbridge were originally one. Edmund (c. 1250-c. 1300), Earl of Cornwall, when a boy, was with
his father—Richard (1209-1272), king of the Romans—at the

Germanic Court, where he saw among the imperial treasures some of Christ's Blood, which had been brought from Greece by Charlemagne. A portion of this was afterward acquired by the earl, who brought it to England in a vessel of gold. This he offered at the altar of the monastery at Hailes, founded by his father near Winchcombe. The fame of the monastery through the possession of so great a relic became very great, and it was the goal of multitudes of pilgrims; and the relic was naturally considered as the most holy thing to swear by. In Chaucer's *Canterbury Tales* he makes the Pardoner to swear:

> *By Goddes precious herte, and by his nailes,*
> *And by the Blood of Christ that is in Hailes.*

When Edmund founded the college of Bonhommes at Ashbridge, he had two-thirds of his gift to Hailes translated to his new foundation.

At the time of the Reformation a statement was made by William Thomas, Clerk of the Council to Edward VI, that the Blood of Hailes was nothing but duck's blood, which was renewed every Saturday. This false statement furnished the source from which some of the historians of the period drew their inspiration. A different account had already been given by the commissioners who were specially sent to examine this relic in the thirtieth year of Henry VIII (1491-1547). They described it to be an unctuous gum, colored, enclosed in a round vessel, garnished and bound on every side with silver; that when within the glass it appeared to be a glistening red like blood, but when taken out, to be yellow, like amber or base gold, and of a sticky substance. The fact was their analytic powers were insufficient to decide what it was.

During some excavating in the ruins of Hailes Abbey in 1900, the foundations of the east end of the church were opened up. A very beautiful apse with five polygonal chapels and two semicircular ambulatories were found, and in the center of this chapel was the base of the shrine of the Holy Blood.

In the twelfth century, Thierry d'Alsace (c. 1099-1168) made a pilgrimage to the Holy Land, whence he returned to Bruges in 1148 with some clots of our Savior's Blood that he had received from King Baldwin III and the patriarch. He built there a chapel in which it should be preserved for the veneration of the faithful, known as the Church of St. Basil, or the Chapel of the Holy Blood. William the Norman, bishop of Tournai, in a manuscript of 1388, attests to have seen and touched with his hands the Holy Blood, which was said to be congealed during the week but liquefied every Friday, from the early morning until the ninth hour, the time of the Passion and death of Christ.

This prelate had a new crystal vessel made, into which he translated the relic. This reliquary, a simple crystal tube, is mounted at either end with goldsmiths' work forming jeweled crowns, from whence issue angels censing.

Fig. 20: Reliquary of the Holy Blood (Bruges).

The châsse, or feretory, into which the reliquary is placed for carrying in processions, is a remarkable piece of work by

Fig. 21: Feretory of the Holy Blood (Bruges).

Jean Crabbe. It was given to the relic in 1617 by the Archduke Albert of Burgundy (1559-1621). It is an elongated hexagonal casket beneath an elaborate canopy, composed entirely of silver gilt, engraved, and covered with pearls, precious stones, and antique cameos.

Beneath smaller canopies are four statuettes in solid gold of the Resurrection, the Blessed Virgin, St. Basil, and St. Donatius. Mary of Burgundy bequeathed her jeweled crown to the relic, and this is placed above the casket but beneath the canopy, only on the day of the annual procession through the city — the Monday after the third of May — a function that is now as popular as such ceremonies were in the medieval ages.

At Boulogne-sur-Mer, a feast of the Precious Blood was observed on July 7. The relic in that town is said to have been sent by Godfrey de Bouillon to the Church of Notre Dame. The beautiful little chapel some distance from the town is supposed to mark the spot where the clergy of Notre Dame first received the relic.

In Mantua is a far-famed relic of the Blood of Christ, which we are assured once issued from a crucifix that was pierced by persons deriding the Christian Faith.

12

THE VOLTO SANTO

The *Volto Santo*, the Holy Face, *le Sudata*, or Veil of St. Veronica, is truly a relic of the Passion to those who accept the beautiful story of St. Veronica. The tradition of the Church is that our Lord, distressed with the sweat of agony on His Via Dolorosa from the house of Pilate to Golgotha, awakened the sympathy of a woman, probably Serapia, who, in defiance of public opinion, which would brand her as immodest, tore off her face veil—by which the female face is always covered in the Orient—and with it wiped the face of her Savior. What a marvelous reward for a small act of loving sympathy was bestowed on that woman when she found that the divine features were imprinted on the cloth.

Serapia—supposed to have been the woman healed of an issue of blood—is said to have been taken to Rome as a witness of Christ's healing power and to have shown the likeness to the emperor.

From this "True Image" (*vera icon*) the woman came to be called Veronica, and the figure on cloth the Vernicle. The latter has since been kept in Rome. It is counted among the four greater relics and is preserved in one of the huge piers that support the dome of St. Peter's. Above an image of St. Veronica at this spot is the following inscription: "That the majesty of the place may becomingly guard Veronica's Likeness of the Savior, Urban VIII, Chief Pontiff, built and adorned this shrine in the year of Jubilee, 1625."

The Vernicle has become so faint by age that the features can scarcely be distinguished, and the pictures, said to be copies of the original, are merely fanciful representations.

13

THE ROBE

The purple robe of majesty placed over the divine shoulders in derision of royalty is confused in the number of holy coats, the tunic, and the seamless robe, which are said to exist. The Holy Coat was kept in a chest in a secret crypt of a church at Galatia, a place mentioned only by Gregory. Twenty-one separate habits are now claimed as the actual garments of our Lord. Some of them—as that at Argenteuil—are known to have been divided for other shrines, thus accounting for various relics. A tunic is preserved at Trier, the city most favored by St. Helena in the cisalpine portion of the Roman Empire. The seamless robe, gambled for

Fig. 22: The Holy Coat, Trier (A Pilgrim's Badge).

by the Roman soldiers, is kept at Argenteuil. They are all in so fragile a condition through the lapse of ages that no adequate examination can be made of them. The medieval history of them is known, but the earlier traditions are more confused than is the case with many other relics.

14

THE HOLY SHROUD

The House of Savoy is proud in its possession of the Holy Shroud in which the body of our Lord was wrapped for the entombment. The *Sancta Sindone*, as it is called, does not hold its claim as the winding-sheet of Christ without sturdy opposition and criticism from the princes of the Church; but its authenticity, which could not be proven and was surrounded by doubt, has received invaluable evidence and support from the modern science of photography.

Where it was kept for the first ten centuries may never be known; this itself has raised doubt as to its genuineness. The first definite notice we have of the "burial cloth" is from pilgrims of the eleventh century, who saw it in the emperor's chapel at Constantinople. In 1150 an English pilgrim speaks of it, and in 1171 William of Tyre (c. 1130-1186) also draws our attention to its presence in that city.

Robert de Clary writes about it in 1203: "And among others there was a monastery called Our Lady Sainte Marie de Blakerne, where were the cloths in which our Lord was wrapped, on which, when one stood straight up, could plainly be seen the figure of our Savior. Since then no one, either Greek or French, can say what became of the cloth after the town was taken."

When, in the face of the infidel, Christian warred against Christian, and the Crusaders were diverted from the Holy Land to the taking and sacking of Constantinople, a Latin king was set on the throne of Byzantium (1201-1205). Garnier de Trainel (c. 1200), bishop of Troyes, took charge of the relics in the Imperial Chapel, but the Shroud is not in the list of those he sent to Europe.

When next we hear of the Shroud, it is in the possession of Geoffrey the First (c. 1300-1356), Count of Charny, who received it in the spoils of war and as a reward for valor in 1353, when he gave it into the custody of the convent of the Abbey of Lirey. In 1355 the count resumed possession of the relic, and it was in the keeping of that house until 1389, when it was returned to the abbey.

During the latter part of the fourteenth century, the bishop of Troyes had a quarrel with the abbot and convent of Lirey and spitefully declared that the linen sheet called the Holy Shroud was a fraud.

The Charny family again had it in 1418 and gave it to the Duke of Savoy who, on June 11, 1502, deposited it in the chapel of Chambery Castle. It rested there until 1532, when the chapel was partially burned and the Shroud was damaged by fire; one corner of the folded linen was consumed, so that when it was opened there were as many holes through it as the number of folds. It was carefully patched by the nuns of St. Claire in 1534, the work occupying them fifteen days; this, and other particulars of the Shroud are recorded in their archives.

The Holy Shroud was conveyed to Turin in 1578, where it has since remained, rolled up in a casket.

When the Shroud was exhibited in 1898, the King of Italy gave permission for it to be photographed, with marvelous results, for the lens revealed much that the eye could not see. Now we can see the portrait of the Lord, the repose of the body as it lay in the grave, and the cruel wounds. St. John, the beloved disciple, who recounts many details omitted by the other Evangelists, tells us: "So he [Joseph of Arimathea] came and took away his body. Nicodemus also, who had at first come to him by night, came bringing a mixture of myrrh and aloes, about a hundred pounds' weight. They took the body of Jesus, and bound it in linen cloths with the spices, as is the burial custom of the Jews" (John 19:38-40).

It is to be remembered that this entombment was hurried, "because of the Jewish day of Preparation, [and] the tomb was close at hand" (John 19:42), and the body was not washed and anointed as was the custom. For this purpose, when the Sabbath was passed, Mary Magdalene, Mary the mother of James, and Salome had brought sweet spices, that they might come and anoint him (Mark 16:1), but they found He had risen.

From the impress of the figure on the Shroud, it is evident that the long cloth has been placed beneath the Lord's body, covered over the head and then continued over the body to the feet, just as the enshrouding is represented in the painting by Giulio Clovio, a pupil of Raphael.

Bearing the above details in mind, we will consider the Shroud of Turin and see how the act of hasty burial has been the means of bequeathing to us the impress of the human form of our Savior.

The most critical examination has put it beyond doubt that it is no painting on the cloth. Then arises the question: How did the figure come to be on it?

The portraiture must have been of a body bathed in urenic perspiration and covered with the sweat of feverish agony; this same body, while still unwashed, must have been covered with the linen heavily imbued with a mixture of oil of myrrh and aloes. The impressions were produced by ammoniacal emanations.

The body remained in contact with the Shroud too short a time to allow of decomposition.

All this is in harmony with a hasty entombment and divesting from the Shroud; and it was on the third day our Lord arose, or within thirty-six hours of the enwrapping.

The impressions are from two surfaces of a human body, the front and the back, on one strip of linen, the two impressions of the head being nearer each other than other parts of the body. All the marks of the wounds are the same as those inflicted on Christ. The spear mark is in the right side of the breast, and the wound of the nail of the left hand — the right is not seen — is in the wrist and not in the palm. The latter has anatomical support, for if the nails were thrust through the palms, the ligaments would tear away when the weight of the body was borne by them. The very fact of this differing from the generally accepted tradition is against the presumption of a forgery.

In addition to the Five Wounds, the blood marks of the scourging on the back and thighs adhere to the Shroud. They all follow one slanting direction, and the appearance of the marks suggests the button-like tipped scourge used by the Roman rather than from rods or a scourge of whipcord.

Another mark on the linen is from behind the right shoulder, where the weight of the cross would rest as our Lord bore it to Golgotha; it was so heavy that He fell, and such a burden would assuredly break the unprotected flesh and cause a bleeding wound.

The Holy Shroud is of very supple linen, still perfectly flexible, quite unlike the early paintings on cloth taken from Egyptian

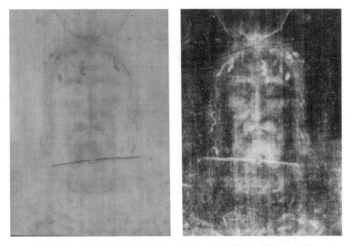

Fig. 23: Detail and negative made from the Holy Shroud (Turin).

sarcophagi or early Christian facecloths. It is now mounted on silk, which was unrolled and stretched within a frame for the last exposition.

SOURCES

Eusebius. *The Life of the Blessed Emperor Constantine: From 306 to 337 A.D.: In Four Books.* The Greek Ecclesiastical Historians of the First Six Centuries of the Christian Era. London: S. Bagster and Sons, 1845.

Fleury, Charles Rohault de. *Mémoire sur les instruments de la Passion De N.-S. J.-C.* Paris: L. Lesort, 1870.

Socrates. *The Ecclesiastical History of Socrates, Comprising a History of the Church, in Seven Books, from the Accession of Constantine, A.D. 305, to the 38th Year of Theodosius II, Including a Period of 140 Years.* Translated from the Greek with some account of the author, and notes selected from Valesius. London: G. Bell, 1879.

BIOGRAPHICAL NOTE

James Charles Wall (1860-1943) was a British author, artist, historian, and antiquarian, well read in the Church Fathers. A Fellow of the Royal Historical Society, he wrote many books, mainly on Church history, and was an early contributor to the Victoria History of the Counties of England magazine. He was somewhat of a mentor to his nephew, the celebrated children's author Charles Williams.

Sophia Institute

Sophia Institute is a nonprofit institution that seeks to nurture the spiritual, moral, and cultural life of souls and to spread the Gospel of Christ in conformity with the authentic teachings of the Roman Catholic Church.

Sophia Institute Press fulfills this mission by offering translations, reprints, and new publications that afford readers a rich source of the enduring wisdom of mankind.

Sophia Institute also operates two popular online Catholic resources: CrisisMagazine.com and CatholicExchange.com.

Crisis Magazine provides insightful cultural analysis that arms readers with the arguments necessary for navigating the ideological and theological minefields of the day. *Catholic Exchange* provides world news from a Catholic perspective as well as daily devotionals and articles that will help you to grow in holiness and live a life consistent with the teachings of the Church.

In 2013, Sophia Institute launched Sophia Institute for Teachers to renew and rebuild Catholic culture through service to Catholic education. With the goal of nurturing the spiritual, moral, and cultural life of souls, and an abiding respect for the role and work of teachers, we strive to provide materials and programs that are at once enlightening to the mind and ennobling to the heart; faithful and complete, as well as useful and practical.

Sophia Institute gratefully recognizes the Solidarity Association for preserving and encouraging the growth of our apostolate over the course of many years. Without their generous and timely support, this book would not be in your hands.

www.SophiaInstitute.com
www.CatholicExchange.com
www.CrisisMagazine.com
www.SophiaInstituteforTeachers.org

Sophia Institute Press® is a registered trademark of Sophia Institute.
Sophia Institute is a tax-exempt institution as defined by the
Internal Revenue Code, Section 501(c)(3). Tax I.D. 22-2548708.